TO BE
YOUNG, GIFTED
AND
BLACK

GIN BRIGGS

TO BE
YOUNG, GIFTED
AND
BLACK

Lorraine Hansberry in Her Own Words

adapted by
Robert Nemiroff

With original drawings and art by Miss Hansberry

and an introduction by
James Baldwin

Prentice-Hall, Inc., Englewood Cliffs, New Jersey

To Be Young, Gifted and Black: Lorraine Hansberry in Her Own Words by Robert Nemiroff.

© Copyright, 1969, by Robert Nemiroff and Robert Nemiroff as Executor of the Estate of Lorraine Hansberry.

"Sweet Lorraine," by James Baldwin, © 1969 by James Baldwin.

SBN 13-923003-3

Library of Congress Catalogue Card Number: 79-80772

To Joy, Nantille, and little Lorraine
in symbolic salute
to the bright, beautiful and brash black young
out of whose ranks Lorraine Hansberry came
in defiance and delight

And for Charlotte
without whom "the commas and periods"
might not have been placed.

Contents

Sweet Lorraine

by James Baldwin

That's the way I always felt about her, and so I won't apologize for calling her that now. *She* understood it: in that far too brief a time when we walked and talked and laughed and drank together, sometimes in the streets and bars and restaurants of the Village, sometimes at her house, sometimes at my house, sometimes gracelessly fleeing the houses of others; and sometimes seeming, for anyone who didn't know us, to be having a knockdown, drag-out battle. We spent a lot of time arguing about history and tremendously related subjects in her Bleecker Street and, later, Waverly Place flat. And often, just when I was certain that she was about to throw me out, as being altogether too rowdy a type, she would stand up, her hands on her hips (for these down-home sessions she always wore slacks) and pick up my empty glass as though she intended to throw it at me. Then she would walk into the kitchen, saying, with a haughty toss of her head, "Really, Jimmy. You ain't *right*, child!" With which stern put-down, she would hand me another drink and launch into a brilliant analysis of just why I wasn't "right." I would often stagger down her stairs as the sun came up, usually in the middle of a paragraph and always in the middle of a laugh. That marvelous laugh. That marvelous face. I loved her, she was my sister and my comrade. Her going did not so much make me lonely as make me realize how lonely we were. We had that respect for each other which perhaps is only felt by people on the same side of the barricades, listening to the accumulating thunder of the hooves of horses and the treads of tanks.

The first time I ever saw Lorraine was at the Actors' Studio, in the winter of '57-58. She was there as an observer of the Workshop Production of *Giovanni's Room*. She sat way up in the bleachers, taking on some of the biggest names in the American theater because she had liked the play and they, in the main, hadn't.

I was enormously grateful to her, she seemed to speak for me; and afterwards she talked to me with a gentleness and generosity never to be forgotten. A small, shy, determined person, with that strength dictated by absolutely impersonal ambition: she was not trying to "make it"—she was trying to keep the faith.

We really met, however, in Philadelphia, in 1959, when *A Raisin in the Sun* was at the beginning of its amazing career. Much has been written about this play; I personally feel that it will demand a far less guilty and constricted people than the present-day Americans to be able to assess it at all; as an historical achievement, anyway, no one can gainsay its importance. What is relevant here is that I had never in my life seen so many black people in the theater. And the reason was that never before, in the entire history of the American theater, had so much of the truth of black people's lives been seen on the stage. Black people ignored the theater because the theater had always ignored them.

But, in *Raisin*, black people recognized that house and all the people in it—the mother, the son, the daughter and the daughter-in-law, and supplied the play with an interpretative element which could not be present in the minds of white people: a kind of claustrophobic terror, created not only by their knowledge of the house but by their knowledge of the streets. And when the curtain came down, Lorraine and I found ourselves in the backstage alley, where she was immediately mobbed. I produced a pen and Lorraine handed me her handbag and began signing autographs. "It only happens once," she said. I stood there and watched. I watched the people, who loved Lorraine for what she had brought to them; and watched Lorraine, who loved the people for what they brought to *her*. It was not, for her, a matter of being admired. She was being corroborated and confirmed. She was wise enough and honest enough to recognize that black American artists are a very special case. One is not merely an artist and one is not judged merely as an artist: the black people crowding around Lorraine, whether or not they considered her an artist, assuredly considered her a witness. This country's concept of art and artists has the effect, scarcely worth mentioning by now, of isolating the artist from the people. One can see the effect of this in the irrelevance of so much of the work produced by celebrated white artists; but the effect of this isolation on a black artist is absolutely fatal. He *is*, already, as a black American citizen, isolated from most of his white countrymen. At the crucial hour, he can hardly look to his artistic peers for help, for they do not know enough about him to be able to correct him. To continue to grow, to remain in touch with himself, he needs the support of that community from which, however, all of the pressures of American life incessantly conspire to remove him. And when he is effectively removed, he falls silent—and the people have lost another hope.

Much of the strain under which Lorraine worked was produced by her knowledge of this reality, and her determined refusal to be destroyed by it. She was a very young woman, with an over-powering vision, and fame had come to her early—she must certainly have wished, often enough, that fame had seen fit to drag its feet a little. For fame and recognition are not synonyms, especially not here, and her fame was to cause her to be criticized very harshly, very loudly, and very often by both black and white people who were unable to believe, apparently, that a really serious intention could be contained in so glamorous a frame. She took it all with a kind of astringent good humor, refusing, for example, even to consider defending herself when she was being accused of being a "slum-lord" because of her family's real-estate holdings in Chicago. I called her during that time, and all she said—with a wry laugh—was, "My God, Jimmy, do you realize you're only the second person who's called me today? And you know how my phone kept ringing *before!*" She was not surprised. She was devoted to the human race, but she was not romantic about it.

When so bright a light goes out so early, when so gifted an artist goes so soon, we are left with a sorrow and wonder which speculation cannot assuage. One is filled for a long time with a sense of injustice as futile as it is powerful. And the vanished person fills the mind, in this or that attitude, doing this or that. Sometimes, very briefly, one hears the exact inflection of the voice, the exact timbre of the laugh—as I have, when watching the dramatic presentation, *To Be Young, Gifted and Black*, and in reading through these pages. But I do not have the heart to presume to assess her work, for all of it, for me, was suffused with the light which was Lorraine. It is possible, for example, that *The Sign in Sidney Brustein's Window* attempts to say too much; but it is also exceedingly probable that it makes so loud and uncomfortable a sound because of the surrounding silence; not many plays, presently, risk being accused of attempting to say too much! Again, Brustein is certainly a very *willed* play, unabashedly didactic; but it cannot, finally, be dismissed or categorized in this way because of the astonishing life of its people. It positively courts being dismissed as old-fashioned and banal and yet has the unmistakable power of turning the viewer's judgment in on himself. *Is all this true or not true?* the play rudely demands; and, unforgivably, leaves us squirming before this question. One cannot quite answer the question negatively, one risks being caught in a lie. But an affirmative answer imposes a new level of responsibility, both for one's conduct and for the fortunes of the American state, and one risks, therefore, the disagreeable necessity of becoming "an insurgent again." For Lorraine made no bones about asserting that art has a purpose, and that its purpose was action: that it contained the "energy which could change things."

It would be good, selfishly, to have her around now, that small, dark girl, with her wit, her wonder, and her eloquent compassion. I've only met one person Lorraine couldn't get through to, and that was the late Bobby Kennedy. And, as the years have passed since that stormy meeting (Lorraine talks about it in these pages, so I won't go into it here) I've very often pondered what she then tried to convey—that a holocaust is no respector of persons; that what, today, seems merely humiliation and injustice for a few, can, unchecked, become Terror for the many, snuffing out white lives just as though they were black lives; that if the American state could not protect the lives of black citizens, then, presently, the entire State would find itself engulfed. And the horses and tanks are indeed upon us, and the end is not in sight. Perhaps it is just as well, after all, that she did not live to see with the outward eye what she saw so clearly with the inward one. And it is not at all farfetched to suspect that what she saw contributed to the strain which killed her, for the effort to which Lorraine was dedicated is more than enough to kill a man.

I saw Lorraine in her hospital bed, as she was dying. She tried to speak, she couldn't. She did not seem frightened or sad, only exasperated that her body no longer obeyed her; she smiled and waved. But I prefer to remember her as she was the last time I saw her on her feet. We were at, of all places, the PEN Club, she was seated, talking, dressed all in black, wearing a very handsome wide, black hat, thin, and radiant. I knew she had been ill, but I didn't know, then, how seriously. I said, "Lorraine, baby, you look beautiful, how in the world do you do it?" She was leaving, I have the impression she was on a staircase, and she turned and smiled that smile and said, "It helps to develop a serious illness, Jimmy!" and waved and disappeared.

Foreword

> "I wish to live because life has within it
> that which is good, that which is beauti-
> ful, and that which is love. Therefore,
> since I have known all of these things, I
> have found them to be reason enough and
> —I wish to live. Moreover, because this
> is so, I wish others to live for generations
> and generations and generations and
> generations."
>
> —Lorraine Hansberry

These words were written not at the end, the culmination of a career, but at the beginning. They were addressed to fellow black writers at a conference on "The Negro Writer and His Roots," March 1, 1959.

Two weeks later the writer's first play, *A Raisin in the Sun*, opened on Broadway.

Two months later Lorraine Hansberry became the youngest American playwright, the fifth woman, the only black writer ever to win the New York Drama Critics Circle Award for "The Best Play of the Year."

Six years later, at the age of 34, Lorraine Hansberry was dead of cancer.

To Be Young, Gifted and Black is the portrait of an individual, the workbook of an artist, and the chronicle of a rebel who cele-brated the human spirit. It is also, I believe, a prophetic chapter in the history of a people and an age.

It is worthy of some emphasis here, therefore, that Lorraine Hansberry's particular view of life did not emerge in one by nature given to celebration, to excessive confidence in the universe or the magnanimity of her fellowmen. What for others may have come with the weight and majesty of profound "existential" revelation—the discovery at some point in life that the universe is not particularly man's friend; that there is an inherent and inevitable tragedy in all men's fate; that there is within every human being an ego which will not be denied without fundamental havoc to himself or those around him; that to fulfill that ego, man is capable of the most incredible acts of transcendence or abasement, sacrifice or aggrandizement, humanity and inhumanity; that even so, our aspirations must ever outstrip our achievements; that we are, in simple fact, all born *dying;* and that, in short, there is a quite impossible, untenable, built-in absurdity to life—all this to her was *assumed:* was already assumed, it seemed to me—though I could neither appreciate nor handle such knowledge at the time—when I first met her as a girl of twenty-one. Had somehow been assumed, I sometimes think—though I know of course this is not possible—from the time she was a very little girl. Perhaps because of her intrinsic sense of vulnerability as a woman in a violent universe; perhaps because of her multifold experience as a *black* woman (*"Life?* Ask those who have tasted of it in pieces rationed out by enemies"); perhaps because of her intuitive view of human frailty and the comedy of errors and compendium of terrors that is the average human life—it never could have occurred to her to think otherwise.

She was a woman of great—some would say inordinate—pride. Yet it is hard to imagine an individual with a truer sense of her own ultimate insignificance in the cosmos. I suspect it was for this reason that one of the symbols she cherished most, from adolescence, was that of the clown. Surrounding her workdesk might be found the symbols of "possibility": photos of Michelangelo's *David*, which to her represented something of man's nobility in the ideal, and of Paul Robeson, and a bust of Einstein, who for her suggested that same nobility in the actual. Yet, privately, she was never more at ease than with clowns. She surrounded herself with clowns. Clown knickknacks, figurines, doo-dads and comic "get well quick" cards. Clown motif pillows, the clowns of Picasso's blue period, her own oil painting of a clown. Clowns and the comic "little folk," grotesques, trolls, *nebishes* and *shmoos* that so tickled her. She considered herself one of these, the little people, the odd-balls, the hapless funny ones. And likened herself to Dinny Dimwit of the comic strips (it pleased her to be told, "Youse is a good girl, Dinny") and to the "little Watching Bird watching you"—with the sneaking suspicion that she looked just a mite like one.

People might describe her as a striking, beautiful woman, but in some part of her she remained—could never really believe she no longer was—the child she had described as "comical... round and... as plain as her brother was angrily handsome." The contrast between the photos in this book and the caricatures she drew of herself (from the stick figure of the child in her grade school autograph book to the adult playwright at her typewriter) is not happenstance.

She was also a being uncommonly possessed of fear. Fear not only of the predictable and anticipated—the everpresent potential for insult, indignity, violence that lurks around any corner, in any casual meeting, and on the hip of any cop in America—but fear, it seemed, of *all* shocks to which flesh is conceivably heir: heights, bridges, tunnels, water, boats, planes, people, the fragility of relationships, the fleeting quality of all life, all beauty. For this woman, who spoke so often of "embracing the stars," it was literally a small physical ordeal, involving a catching of the breath and tightening of the muscles, simply to get on an elevator. (Sometimes, unaccountably, to those who could not know why—and she was much too proud to tell—she would walk the three or four flights, or make a joke of it; more often she faced down her hobgoblins in silence.) Her dread of hospitals was such that, until the hour her own illness struck, she had been, with only one exception that I can recall, unable to bring herself to enter their antiseptic corridors and unconvincingly cheerful rooms even to visit close friends. Yet this same woman was not afraid, in her last year, between lengthening sojourns in and out of hospitals, to ask of herself:

> Do I remain a revolutionary? Intellectually—without a doubt. But am I prepared to give my body to the struggle or even my *comforts?* . . .

That was in the summer of 1964, a time of heightening confrontation in the Deep South, of the "Mississippi Summer Project," police dogs in Birmingham and cattleprods in the Carolinas; the year that Chaney, Schwerner and Goodman (among others less well celebrated) answered the same question for themselves, and for all time, in a station-wagon for which Lorraine Hansberry had helped to raise the funds. Carrying a portable typewriter back and forth from home to hospital, and a new initialed dispatch case jammed with photos from the front lines, she completed the revisions for her second play, *The Sign in Sidney Brustein's Window,* scheduled to open that fall, and simultaneously, the text she had promised for SNCC's epic book of photographs: *The Movement: Documentary of a Struggle for Equality*. Her journal records this answer to the question she had posed: "I think when I get my health back I shall go into the South to find out what kind of revolutionary I am."

In *Sidney Brustein* she amplified in depth the nature of her commitment. Critic Emory Lewis has described a passage from that play as containing "perhaps the finest lines in modern American dramatic literature":

> I care. I care about it all. It takes too much energy *not* to care. Yesterday I counted twenty-six gray hairs on the top of my head all from trying *not* to care.... The *why* of why we are here is an intrigue for adolescents; the *how* is what must command the living. Which is why I have lately become an insurgent again.

For Lorraine Hansberry insurgency was a necessity, an essence of the artist. A necessity inseparable from her blackness, her womanhood, her humanism.

Nothing ever said about her, for example, more amused or alternately struck such sparks of wrath from her than the notion that she was "a writer who happened to be a Negro." (An early, admiring interviewer in *The New York Times* intended that misquote as a compliment; there was a hot exchange of letters concerning it, but the designation lingered because it was in those days what most Americans were only too eager to hear.) The view of life which permeates these pages was inextricably rooted in the collective history of a people with a special vantage point on life, a vantage point that made it difficult—in her eyes, unseemly and impossible—to take refuge in the comforting illusions—or underlying assumptions—of our society. But if blackness brought pain, it was also a source of strength, renewal and inspiration, a window on the potentials of the human race. For if Negroes could survive America, then there was hope for the human race indeed. And if life was, in fact, an absurdity, then the only thing that remained, the only acceptable choice, was for man to "do what the apes never will—*impose* the reason for life on life":

> ...*Despair?* Did someone say *despair* was a question in the world? Well then, listen to the sons of those who have known little else if you wish to know the resiliency of this thing you

would so quickly resign to mythhood, this thing called the human spirit.

And that is why, looking back, it is not surprising (although, again, as with so many aspects of Lorraine, it was impossible for me to fathom the special significance of her words at the time, in fact, I hardly noted them) that as early as 1961, at the height of health and success, she had already taken the measure of the enemy that was waiting for her. It was in a casual piece for *Playbill* magazine, in which she recalled our meeting a woman the previous summer "who had lived a purposeful and courageous life and who was then dying of cancer," a woman who "had also been of radical viewpoint all her life":

> ...one of those people who energetically believe that the world *can* be changed for the better and spend their lives trying to do just that. And that was the way she thought of cancer; she absolutely refused to award it the stature of tragedy, a devastating instance of the brooding doom and inexplicable absurdity of human destiny....
> But for this remarkable woman it was a matter of nature in imperfection, implying, as always, work for man to do. It was an *enemy*, but a palpable one with shape and effect and source; and if it existed it could be destroyed.

All this, then, will suggest the extent to which the affirmation that defined her work was indeed the deliberate *imposition* of a conscious view of life, of the human will over nature—including her own nature. "The supreme test of technical skill and creative imagination," she wrote in summing up her hopes for American art in coming years, "is the depth of art it requires to render the infinite varieties of the human spirit—which invariably hangs *between* despair and joy."

It was this test that she set for herself in her life and her work. And it is this test, I believe, that will provide the ultimate measure of her achievement.

The substance of that achievement, the work she left, rests in three file cabinets in the office in which she wrote, and where this is being written. In quantity, range and degree of completion it is a body of work beyond anything that anyone—myself included, involved though I was in so much of it—could have anticipated at the time she died.

Among her manuscripts is *Les Blancs*, four years in the writing, which it seems to me now in the light of all that has happened since —and the choices yet remaining before us—will quite possibly stand as her major work. An exploration in depth of the making of a black revolutionary, it is to be produced on Broadway and will be published next year. A second forthcoming volume will contain three shorter plays, including *The Drinking Gourd* and *What Use Are Flowers*. A collection of her non-dramatic works, including a novel in progress, will be published in one or several volumes by Prentice-Hall under the title *Posthumously: In Defense of Life*. The work of sifting and editing her manuscripts and papers—drafts and partial drafts of other stage plays, screenplays, fiction, poetry, essays, speeches, memoirs, journals and her considerable correspondence—has only just begun.

To Be Young, Gifted and Black, then, is not *all* of Lorraine Hansberry, but a small representative sampling, a cross-section selected and shaped with a particular purpose in mind: to relate the artist to the person, and place the parts within the context of the whole in such fashion as to enable the words she left to tell her story without intrusion or comment, explanation or footnotes of any kind. It is a self-portrait, in that the words, experiences, characters and creations—including all the artwork which accompanies the text—are the artist's own. But it is also an adaptation, a portrait rendered through the perspective of another's eyes. And therefore it takes a somewhat novel form: biography and autobiography, part fact, part fiction, an act of creation and re-creation utilizing first-person materials as well as, inferentially, autobiographical projections of herself in her characters.

In the process, some minor liberties have been taken. Speeches, letters, journal entries, transcripts of interviews, miscellaneous observations have, in some instances, been condensed and consolidated. Sometimes where one idea has been variously stated in different contexts, the most felicitous phrasing has been chosen for clarity's sake. Scenes from the plays have been pulled together, when required, to make dramatic or thematic units that could stand on their own outside the original contexts. Some slight shifting of dates has been made to assist the unfolding structure. And necessary editing has, of course, occurred.

At all times the object has been to present the essence of the person and her ideas—leaving amplification to the definitive editions of her works that are to follow.

Croton-on-Hudson   ROBERT NEMIROFF

Acknowledgments

"...This last should be the least difficult—since there are so many who think as I do—"

The wish could only have come from one who thought as she did: that simple audacious expression of faith which marks the conclusion of this book that—"if anything should happen"—somehow the commas and periods would be placed, the thoughts completed, the work go on. An extravagant hope, wistfully improbable and, as usual—as the years have proved—unerringly accurate.

It is not possible, for example, to complete this book without a word about Charlotte Zaltzberg, my secretary, friend and editorial assistant for three years, who, without stint or quarter, day, night and often enough weekends, has worked creatively and critically (a role for which she is eminently suited) as well as on the most mundane mechanical tasks (for which she is eminently not) to make this book and the play of the same name, and all the others that are to follow, realities.

But Charlotte was not, of course, alone. It is a simple, eloquent fact—and a particular tribute that would, I think, have moved Lorraine perhaps beyond any other—that literally hundreds have helped in these years to preserve and pass on the words she left. They include many who, like Charlotte, never met Lorraine Hansberry, and others who were amongst her closest friends and comrades; some who indeed "think" as she did—and even some who do not. Each has helped in ways large and small, and collectively they are far too many to enumerate here. None would require in any case, I suspect, formal recognition for personal involvement so freely tendered. Nonetheless, I trust that each will share a bit more intensely in the pleasures and satisfactions of this book for having helped to bring it into existence.

At the same time there are those whose contributions have been so sizable, either directly in terms of the work itself, or indirectly in their assistance or encouragement to me, that of necessity their names cannot be omitted from these pages. At the risk, therefore, of (I fear) inevitably overlooking someone to whom I am especially grateful in the rush of completing this manuscript (which, like most manuscripts, is overdue at this writing), I should like to thank the following now:

- My parents, Mae and Motya, who loved Lorraine as their own; my brother Leo, who was the first to teach me most of what I know about writing and the human values we shared with Lorraine; and Mili, my sister, who began this work at my side, gave of her great gifts unremittingly, and sustained it through the most difficult times;
- Seymour Baldash, Alan Bomser, Bob Brittan, Joe Burstin, Jim MacDevitt, Lyle Marshall, and Judd Woldin, whose dedication and friendship have gone so far beyond the purely professional;
- Howard Hausman, the first agent I ever met who proved not a "necessary evil," but a true friend of art;
- James Baldwin, who believed and brought his special eloquence to these pages;
- Kenneth Clark, Morris and Abby Colman, Alvin Epstein, Madeline Gilford, Albert Handy, Inga Irving, Lillian and Frank Jaros, Mary Kaplan, the J. M. Kaplan Fund, Edith and Samuel Kamen, John and Grace Killens, Sidney Kingsley, Lynn and Burton Lane, Judy and Irving Lerner, Viveca Lindfors, Audrey Miller, David and Judy Nemiroff, George Nicolau, Frederick D. Patterson, Rabbi Michael Robinson, Norma Rodgers, Raymond Rubinow, Bayard Rustin, Dr. Abram Sachar, Diana Sands, Dore Schary, Harold Scott, Dorothy Secules, Joseph Stein, George Tabori, Cora and Peter Weiss, Abe and Debbie Weisburd, for giving of themselves so freely and sweetly;
- Frank Millspaugh and the staff and volunteer workers of the embattled but eternally venturesome WBAI: the nature of their unique contribution is indicated in the background *Postscript* at the end of the book—as are the names of the distinguished artists who gave so magnificently, freely and lovingly of their time and talent to the germinal first public presentation of many of the words in this book;
- *And seven for whom no words can suffice:* Ossie Davis and Ruby Dee, Burt and Art D'Lugoff, Estelle Frank, Edith Gordon and Ray Larsen.

To my colleagues these past six months at the Cherry Lane Theatre who helped to bring the stage adaptation of *To Be Young, Gifted and Black* to life, I should like to express my profound gratitude: Harry Belafonte, Chiz Schultz and Edgar Lansbury, the original producers; Ray Larsen and Burt D'Lugoff, whose absolute faith and generosity are, above all, responsible for the success it has become; Gene Frankel, who so brilliantly helped to put the flesh on the bones of the script I brought him; and our uncommonly gifted cast—both those who first breathed the breath of life into it, and those who have continued with such distinction in the roles (their names appear in the *Note on the Stage Play* at the back of the book, along with those who created the imaginative physical and musical settings for the production.) And a special word of appreciation is also due Gigi Cascio and Eastern Hale; Joe Burstin and Joe Beruh; Milly Schoenbaum; Al Isaacs, Jewel Howard and Rob Bauer; Max Eisen and Cheryl Sue Dolby; Michael Dembo and all the others in the company—for yeoman service and dedication behind the scenes.

For permission to reprint material which has previously appeared elsewhere, I am deeply grateful to Random House, publishers of *A Raisin in the Sun* and *The Sign in Sidney Brustein's Window*, and to the editors and publishers of the following publications: *Playbill* ("On Summer"); *Village Voice* ("Thoughts on Genet, Mailer and the New Paternalism"); *Theatre Arts* ("Me Tink Me Hear Sounds in De Night"); *Mademoiselle* ("Quo Vadis"); *National Guardian* ("The Black Revolution and the White Backlash"); *Show Magazine* ("The Shakespearean Experience"); *The Urbanite* ("Images and Essences/1961 Dialogue with an Uncolored Egghead Containing Wholesome Intentions and Some Sass"); *WFMT Fine Arts Guide* ("An Interview with Lorraine Hansberry by Studs Terkel"); *Vogue*, "People Are Talking About." I'm also indebted to Harold Ober Associates Incorporated for permission to reprint an excerpt from Langston Hughes' poem "Montage of a Dream Deferred," and to St. Martin's Press and Mrs. Sean O'Casey for permission to reprint excerpts from *Juno and the Paycock* by Sean O'Casey.

xxi

As these words are being written, it is almost seven fateful years to the day that I heard Lorraine Hansberry, from the rostrum of Town Hall, speak the words to be found in the concluding portions of this book—about the Black Revolution and the "white backlash," peace, Viet Nam, and the way ahead. It is our tragedy that so few could recognize then what is obvious now. At this hour, therefore, I should like to express my particular appreciation and gratitude to those of my fellow Americans who, while I was home at my desk, were out in the streets, in the black movement, the peace movement, the youth movement—heroes of the ghetto and the campus who, in whole or even in tragically fractured part, have helped to maintain the continuity that one day may give Lorraine's vision life.

And lastly, a word for my wife, Jewell, who for two years has made this work, and all my life, her own—understanding its importance when others would have doubted and even I was led to hesitate. Without her profound love and belief, the wisdom and joy with which she filled the hours in which this book took shape, and studied its pages, neither it, nor I, could be as you find us now.

R. N.

PROLOGUE
Measure
Him Right,
Child

1.

Bare stage. An old man enters, looks out at the audience, wanders about for several moments trying to find his bearings and at last sits, his back largely to the audience. He removes a hard-boiled egg from his pocket, cracks it, salts it and is about to bite when suddenly he turns.

HERMIT

You might as well know that you do not frighten me. I shall eat my breakfast and be content whether you stay or go. And when you recover your tongues, I will accept your directions. I should like, with your consideration, to reach some outpost of, if you will forgive the reference, "civilization" by nightfall.

(*He turns his back, to eat, then suddenly, struck with the thought*)

I wonder if you might tell an old man something. If only I might persuade you quite what it would mean to me. You see, I should very much like to know—

(*Deep pause*)

—what *time* it is. You think that's silly, don't you; yes, I rather thought you would. That a chap might go off and hide himself in the woods for twenty years and then come out and ask, "What time is it?"

(*He laughs*)

But you see, one of the reasons I left is because I could no longer stand the dominion of time in the lives of men and the things that they did with it and to it and, indeed, that they let it do to them. And so, to escape time, I threw my watch away. I even made a ceremony of it. I was on a train over a bridge . . . and I held it out the door and dropped it. Quite like—

(*He gestures, remembering*)

—this. But do you know the very first thing I absolutely had a compulsion to know once I got into the forest? I wanted to know what time it was. Certainly I had no appointments to keep—but I *longed* to know the hour of the day. Of

3

course, there is no such thing as an hour, it is merely something that men have labeled so—but I longed to have that label at my command again.

I never did achieve that. Ultimately I gave up minutes, hours too; ah, but I kept up with the days! It got to be a matter of rejoicing that the seasons came when I knew they would. Or, at least that's how it was for the first fifteen years. Because, naturally, I lost track. I accumulated a backlog of slipped days which, apparently, ran into months because one year, quite suddenly, it began to snow when I expected the trees to bud. Somewhere I had mislaid a warm autumn for a chilly spring . . . I almost died that year; I had lost a season.

Consequently, among other things, I no longer know how old I am. I was fifty-eight when I went into the woods. And now I am either seventy-eight or perhaps more than eighty years old. That's why I have come out of the woods. I am afraid men invent time*pieces;* they do not invent time. We may give time its dimensions and meaning, we may make it worthless or important or absurd or crucial. But ultimately I am afraid it has a value of its own.

It is time for me to die, and I have come out to see what men have been doing, and now that I am back, more than anything else just now, you see, I should very much like to know: what time it is. . . .

> *The* HERMIT *freezes, remaining in position as the* LIGHTS *dim slightly.*

2.

PROJECTION of LORRAINE HANSBERRY and her recorded voice in the midst of an interview.

I suppose I think that the highest gift that man has is art, and I am audacious enough to think of myself as an artist— that there is both joy and beauty and illumination and communion between people to be achieved through the dissection of personality. That's what I want to do. I want to reach a little closer to the world, which is to say to people, and see if we can share some illuminations together about each other.

I happen to believe that most people—and this is where I differ from many of my contemporaries, or at least as they express themselves—I think that virtually every human being is dramatically interesting. Not only is he dramatically interesting, he is a creature of stature whoever he is. . . .

3.

> LIGHT UP *on* WALTER LEE
> YOUNGER, *a lean intense young*
> *black man in his middle thirties,*
> *in pajamas or bathrobe, and his*
> *wife* RUTH, *in housecoat. The*
> HERMIT *remains.*

WALTER

You look young this morning, baby.

RUTH
(*Indifferently*)

Yeah?

WALTER

Just for a second—stirring them eggs. It's gone now—just for a second it was—you looked real young again.
(*Then, drily*)
It's gone now. You look like yourself again.

RUTH
(*Setting his eggs before him*)
Man, if you don't shut up and leave me alone.

WALTER

First thing a man ought to learn in life is not to make love to no colored woman first thing in the morning. You all some evil people at eight o'clock in the morning.

RUTH
(*Wearily*)
Oh, Walter Lee . . .

WALTER
(*Rising and coming to her and standing over her*)
"Oh, Walter Lee"! You tired, ain't you? Tired of everything.
Me, the boy, the way we live—but you wouldn't do nothing
to help, would you?

RUTH
Walter, please leave me alone.

WALTER
A man needs for a woman to back him up . . .

RUTH
Walter, eat your eggs, they gonna be cold.

WALTER
(*Straightening up and looking off*)
That's it. There you are. Man say to his woman: I got me a
dream. His woman say: eat your eggs.
(*With slowly rising anger*)
Man say: I got to take hold of this here world, baby! And a
woman will say: Eat your eggs and go to work.
(*Passionately now*)
Man say: I got to change my life, I'm choking to death, baby!
And his woman say—
(*In utter anguish as he brings his fists down on his thighs*)
—Your eggs is getting cold! That is just what is wrong with
the colored woman in this world . . . Don't understand
about building their men up and making 'em feel like they
somebody. Like they can do something.

RUTH
(*Drily, but to hurt*)
There *are* colored men who do things . . .

WALTER
No thanks to the colored woman.

RUTH
Well, being a colored woman, I guess I can't help myself none.
Eat your eggs, Walter.

WALTER
DAMN MY EGGS . . . DAMN ALL THE EGGS THAT
EVER WAS!

> THEY *freeze, remain in position as
> the* LIGHT *dims slightly.*

4.

> LIGHT UP *on* ZEB DUDLEY, *a poor
> white farmer.* WALTER, RUTH *and
> the* HERMIT *remain.*

ZEB
(*With true feeling, not caricature—the
burning intensity of self-justification*)
Don't talk to me about right and wrong, Preacher—a man does
with his hands what he has to! Or mebbe you think God
made these hands to sit idle while he watches his babies turn
the color of death? Well, I ain't never found nothin' fine
and noble 'bout bein' no dirt-eater. I don't aim to end up
no red-neck cracker the rest of my life, out there scrappin'
on that near-gravel, trying to get a little corn to grow, allus
watchin' somebody else's plantation gettin' closer and closer
to my land! I'm a *white man*, Preacher! And I'm going to
drive slaves for Everett Sweet, and he's gonna pay me for it,
and this time next year Zeb Dudley aims to own *himself*
some slaves and be a man—you hear!

> ZEB *freezes, dims slightly.*

5.

> LIGHT UP *on* IRIS BRUSTEIN, *of
> gamin slenderness and vivacity,
> her hair at the moment elaborately
> coiffed, in her hands a large,
> elegantly lettered "Golden Girl
> Curl" box.*

IRIS
(*Defiantly—a woman fighting for compo-
sure*)
What am I *selling*, Sidney? What do I *do* in the commercial?
Home permanents! . . . No, it *isn't* what they've used on

me. Don't be funny, this head has been in and out of all the booths in Mr. Lionel's for the last two-and-one-half hours . . . no, Sid, that certainly is not what I am going to tell them! I am going to tell all the little housewifies that I just rolled it up on Golden Girl Curl—

> (*Holding up the box, she assumes the manner of a* TV *mannequin, with the slightest edge of hysteria just beneath the surface of her kidding*)

—and rollers, using my magic Golden Girl Curl Box to hold everything just so. Which, you understand, is one of the main features of Golden Girl Curl Home Permanent . . . the box it comes in—

> (*Enunciating with contempt*)

Yes! The box it comes in!

> (*She opens it grandly—the bottom falls out and so do the rollers. She hurls it to the floor*)

Which also does not work!

> (*Wheeling, crying, shrieking*)

It's a job, Sidney! They do not pay you one hundred dollars an hour for hauling hamburgers at Hamlines. They do pay it for pretending that there is some difference between Golden Girl Curl and Wonder Curl, or between Wonder Curl and Home Perma Pearl, so what the hell do you want from me?

> (*Precisely now in the manner of a defensive child*)

Well, it *does* work! It does work enough to justify it! They just send you to the hairdressers to play safe. They have to have everything just so when they tape things for television, Sidney. You don't realize how expensive it is to tape something. All those lights and cameras and technicians . . . they can't have your hair falling down from some–crappy old home permanent just when they're ready to shoot! . . .

> IRIS *freezes, dims slightly.*

6.

> MUSIC UP—*hot and low and intense.* LIGHT *on* GLORIA PARODUS, *glass in hand, snapping her fingers and undulating a little to the beat. The* OTHERS *remain.*

GLORIA

I was on this date once. He had a book of reproductions by
Goya. And there was this one—an etching, I think. Have
you ever seen it? There's this woman, a Spanish peasant
woman, and she's standing like this—reaching out. And what
she's reaching out for are the teeth of a dead man. A man
who'd been hanged. And she is rigid with—revulsion, but
. . . she wants his teeth because it said in the book that in
those days people thought that the teeth of the dead were
good luck. Can you imagine that? The things people think
they have to do? To *survive* in this world?
(*She stops dancing, abruptly sobering*)
Some day I'm going to buy that print. It's all about my
life . . .

GLORIA *freezes, dims slightly.*

7.

LIGHT UP *on* LENA YOUNGER—
MAMA—*a strong full-bodied black
woman in her early sixties. The*
OTHERS *remain.*

MAMA

You—you mourning your brother? You feeling like you better
than he is today? What you tell him a minute ago? That he
wasn't a man? Yes? You give him up for me? You done
wrote his epitaph too—like the rest of the world? Well, who
give you the privilege? . . . Child, when do you think is
the time to love somebody the most: when they done good
and made things easy for everybody? Well then, you ain't
through learning—because that ain't the time at all. It's when
he's at his lowest and can't believe in hisself 'cause the world
done whipped him so. When you starts measuring somebody, measure him *right*, child, measure him right. Make
sure you done taken into account what hills and valleys he
come through before he got to wherever he is . . .

MAMA *freezes, dims slightly.*

9

8.

Against the living backdrop of this gallery of characters, onto the stage now strides a young black woman of twenty-eight, in her hands a speech—to which she does not, however, refer.

PLAYWRIGHT

Good evening. I am very pleased to have been invited to be a part of this program, and—

(*Smiling*)

—and I hope it isn't premature. That is, this *is* a Writers' Conference, a Negro Writers Conference to be exact; I am, clearly, a Negro—but I'm not sure yet how much of a writer I am. I suppose I have been invited because my first play will be opening soon (that is, *if* they give us a theater). I think I like it, but I've no idea what the public will think of it. Still, for the moment, let's presume I am a writer.

(*Now she refers to the typed speech she has been carrying*)

I must share with you a part of a conversation I had with a young New York intellectual a year ago in my living room in Greenwich Village. He was a young man I had known, not well but for a number of years, who was, by way of description, an ex-Communist, a scholar and a serious student of philosophy and literature, and whom I consider to possess quite a fine and exceptionally alert mind. In any case, he and I had wandered conversationally into the realm of discussion which haunts the days of humankind everywhere: the destruction or survival of the human race.

"Why," he said to me, "are you so sure the human race *should* go on? You do not believe in a prior arrangement of life on this planet. You know perfectly well that the *reason* for survival does not exist in nature!"

I was somewhat taken aback by the severity that this kind of feeling has apparently reached among a generation that presumably should be lying on its back in the spring woods somewhere, contemplating lyrics of love and daring and the wonder of wild lilies.

I answered him the only way I could: that man is unique in the universe, the only creature who has in fact the power to transform the universe. Therefore, it did not seem unthinkable to me that man might just do what the apes never will—*impose* the reason for life on life. That is what I said to my friend. I wish to live because life has within it that which is good, that which is beautiful, and that which is love. Therefore, since I have known all of these things, I have found them to be reason enough and—I wish to live. Moreover, because this is so, I wish others to live for generations and generations and generations and generations.

I was born on the Southside of Chicago. I was born black and a female. I was born in a depression after one world war, and came into my adolescence during another. While I was still in my teens the first atom bombs were dropped on human beings at Nagasaki and Hiroshima, and by the time I was twenty-three years old my government and that of the Soviet Union had entered actively into the worst conflict of nerves in human history—the Cold War.

I have lost friends and relatives through cancer, lynching and war. I have been personally the victim of physical attack which was the offspring of racial and political hysteria. I have worked with the handicapped and seen the ravages of congenital diseases that we have not yet conquered because we spend our time and ingenuity in far less purposeful wars. I see daily on the streets of New York, street gangs and prostitutes and beggars; I know people afflicted with drug addiction and alcoholism and mental illness; I have, like all of you, on a thousand occasions seen indescribable displays of man's very real inhumanity to man; and I have come to maturity, as we all must, knowing that greed and malice, indifference to human misery and, perhaps above all else, ignorance—the prime ancient and persistent enemy of man—abound in this world.

I say all of this to say that one cannot live with sighted eyes and feeling heart and not know and react to the miseries which afflict this world.

I have given you this account so that you know that what I write is not based on the assumption of idyllic possibilities or innocent assessments of the true nature of life—but, rather, my own personal view that, posing one against the other, I think that the human race does command its own destiny and that that destiny can eventually embrace the stars. . . .

11

PART ONE

"I Wish to Live..."

I ⟡

CHICAGO:
Southside Summers

EDWARD J. BARRETT

COUNTY CLERK

BUREAU OF VITAL STATISTICS—130 NORTH WELLS STREET
CHICAGO 6, ILLINOIS

STATE OF ILLINOIS
Department of Public Health - Division of Vital Statistics

ORIGINAL

CERTIFICATE OF BIRTH

Registered No. 21385

Registration Dist. No. 3104

Primary Dist. No. 3104

1. PLACE OF BIRTH
County of Cook
Chicago
Street and Number, No. 16 W 36th

Ward Provident Hospital
(If birth occurred in hospital or institution, give its name instead of street and number.)

2. FULL NAME OF CHILD: Loraine Hansberry

3. Sex of Child	4. Twin, Triplet, or other?	5. Number in order of birth	6. Legitimate?	7. Date of birth
Female	(To be answered only in the event of plural births)		yes	May 19, 1930

FATHER

8. Full Name: Carl A. Hansberry
9. Residence (P.O. Address): 5330 Calumet ave
10. Color: negro B   11. Age at last birthday: 33 years
12. Birthplace (City or Place): Glaston Miss
13. Occupation (Nature of Industry): U.S. Depty marshall

MOTHER

14. Full Maiden Name: Nannie Perry
15. Residence (P.O. Address): 5330 Calumet ave
16. Color: negro B   17. Age at last birthday: 32 years
18. Birthplace (City or Place): Columbia Tenn
19. Occupation (Nature of Industry): Ward Committeeman

20. Number of children of this mother.
(Taken as of time of birth of child herein certified and including this child.)
(a) Born alive and now living 4   (b) Born alive but now dead 0   (c) Stillborn 0

What treatment was given child's eyes at birth?

21. CERTIFICATE OF ATTENDING PHYSICIAN OR MIDWIFE

I hereby certify that I attended the birth of this child, who was BORN ALIVE 7 8 2 4 P.M., on the date above stated.
22. (Signature) M.D.
Address 4700 Saw Park ... Telephone Drex 2635
Date Certificate Signed

24. Filed MAY 28 1930

STATE OF ILLINOIS,
County of Cook, } ss.

I, EDWARD J. BARRETT, County Clerk of the County of Cook, in the State aforesaid, and Keeper of the Records and Files of said County, do hereby certify that the attached is a true and correct copy of the original Record on file, all of which appears from the records and files in my office.

IN WITNESS WHEREOF, I have hereunto set my hand and affixed the Seal of the County of Cook, at my office in the City of Chicago, in said County.

Edward J. Barrett
County Clerk

1.

For some time now—I think since I was a child—I have been possessed of the desire to put down the stuff of my life. That is a commonplace impulse, apparently, among persons of massive self-interest; sooner or later we all do it. And, I am quite certain, there is only one internal quarrel: how much of the truth to tell? How much, how much, how much! It *is* brutal, in sober uncompromising moments, to reflect on the comedy of concern we all enact when it comes to our precious images!

Even so, when such vanity as propels the writing of such memoirs is examined, certainly one would wish at least to have some boast of social serviceability on one's side. I shall set down in these pages what shall seem to me to be the truth of my life and essences . . . which are to be found, first of all, on the Southside of Chicago, where I was born. . . .

2.

All travelers to my city should ride the elevated trains that race along the back ways of Chicago. The lives you can look into!

I think you could find the tempo of my people on their back porches. The honesty of their living is there in the shabbiness. Scrubbed porches that sag and look their danger. Dirty gray wood steps. And always a line of white and pink clothes scrubbed so well, waving in the dirty wind of the city.

My people are poor. And they are tired. And they are determined to live.

Our Southside is a place apart: each piece of our living is a protest.

3.

I was born May 19, 1930, the last of four children.

Of love and my parents there is little to be written: their relationship to their children was utilitarian. We were fed and housed and dressed and outfitted with more cash than our associates and that was all. We were also vaguely taught certain vague absolutes: that we were better than no one but infinitely superior to everyone; that we were the products of the proudest and most mistreated of the races of man; that there was nothing enormously difficult about life; that one *succeeded* as a matter of course.

17

Life was not a struggle—it was something that one *did*. One won an argument because, if facts gave out, one invented them—with color! The only sinful people in the world were dull people. And, above all, there were two things which were never to be betrayed: the family and the race. But of love, there was nothing ever said.

If we were sick, we were sternly, impersonally and carefully nursed and doctored back to health. Fevers, toothaches were attended to with urgency and importance; one always felt *important* in my family. Mother came with a tray to your room with the soup and Vick's salve or gave the enemas in a steaming bathroom. But we were not fondled, any of us—head held to breast, fingers about that head—until we were grown, all of us, and my father died.

At his funeral I at last, in my memory, saw my mother hold her sons that way, and for the first time in her life my sister held me in her arms I think. We were not a loving people: we were passionate in our hostilities and affinities, but the caress embarrassed us.

We have changed little. . . .

4.

Seven years separated the nearest of my brothers and sisters and myself; I wear, I am sure, the earmarks of that familial station to this day. Little has been written or thought to my knowledge about children who occupy that place: the last born separated by an uncommon length of time from the next youngest. I suspect we are probably a race apart.

The last born is an object toy which comes in years when brothers and sisters who are seven, ten, twelve years older are old enough to appreciate it rather than poke out its eyes. They do not mind diapering you the first two years, but by the time you are five you are a pest that has to be attended to in the washroom, taken to the movies and "sat with" at night. You are not a person—you are a nuisance who is not particular fun any more. Consequently, you swiftly learn to play alone. . . .

5.

My childhood Southside summers were the ordinary city kind, full of the street games which other rememberers have turned into fine ballets these days, and rhymes that anticipated what some people insist on calling modern poetry:

Oh, Mary Mack, Mack, Mack
With the silver buttons, buttons, buttons
All down her back, back, back.
She asked her mother, mother, mother
For fifteen cents, cents, cents
To see the elephant, elephant, elephant
Jump the fence, fence, fence.
Well, he jumped so high, high, high
'Til he touched the sky, sky, sky
And he didn't come back, back, back
'Til the Fourth of Ju—ly, ly, ly!

I remember skinny little Southside bodies by the fives and tens
of us panting the delicious hours away·
"May I?"
And the voice of authority: "Yes, you may—you may take one
giant step."
One drew in all one's breath and tightened one's fist and pulled
the small body against the heavens, stretching, straining all the
muscles in the legs to make—one giant step.
It is a long time. One forgets the reason for the game. (For
children's games are always explicit in their reasons for being. To
play is to win something. Or not to be "it." Or to be high pointer,
or outdoer or, sometimes—just *the winner*. But after a time one
forgets.)
Why was it important to take a small step, a teeny step, or the
most desired of all—one GIANT step?
A giant step *to where?*

6.

Evenings were spent mainly on the back porches where screen
doors slammed in the darkness with those really very special sum-
mertime sounds. And, sometimes, when Chicago nights got too
steamy, the whole family got into the car and went to the park
and slept out in the open on blankets. Those were, of course, the
best times of all because the grownups were invariably reminded
of having been children in the South and told the best stories then.
And it was also cool and sweet to be on the grass and there was
usually the scent of freshly cut lemons or melons in the air. Daddy
would lie on his back, as fathers must, and explain about how men
thought the stars above us came to be and how far away they were.
I never did learn to believe that anything could be as far away
as *that*. Especially the stars. . . .

7.

The man that I remember was an educated soul, though I think now, looking back, that it was as much a matter of the physical bearing of my father as his command of information and of thought that left that impression upon me. I know nothing of the "assurance of kings" and will not use that metaphor on account of it. Suffice it to say that my father's enduring image in my mind is that of a man whom kings might have imitated and properly created their own flattering descriptions of. A man who always seemed to be doing something brilliant and/or unusual to such an extent that to be doing something brilliant and/or unusual was the way I assumed fathers behaved.

He digested the laws of the State of Illinois and put them into little booklets. He invented complicated pumps and railroad devices. He could talk at length on American history and private enterprise (to which he utterly subscribed). And he carried his head in such a way that I was quite certain that there was nothing he was afraid of. Even writing this, how profoundly it shocks my inner senses to realize suddenly that *my father*, like all men, must have known *fear*. . . .

8.

April 23, 1964

To the Editor,
The New York Times:

With reference to civil disobedience and the Congress of Racial Equality stall-in:

. . . My father was typical of a generation of Negroes who believed that the "American way" could successfully be made to work to democratize the United States. Thus, twenty-five years ago, he spent a small personal fortune, his considerable talents, and many years of his life fighting, in association with NAACP attorneys, Chicago's "restrictive covenants" in one of this nation's ugliest ghettoes.

That fight also required that our family occupy the disputed property in a hellishly hostile "white neighborhood" in which, literally, howling mobs surrounded our house. One of their missiles almost took the life of the then eight-year-old signer

20

of this letter. My memories of this "correct" way of fighting white supremacy in America include being spat at, cursed and pummeled in the daily trek to and from school. And I also remember my desperate and courageous mother, patrolling our house all night with a loaded German luger, doggedly guarding her four children, while my father fought the respectable part of the battle in the Washington court.

The fact that my father and the NAACP "won" a Supreme Court decision, in a now famous case which bears his name in the lawbooks, is—ironically—the sort of "progress" our satisfied friends allude to when they presume to deride the more radical means of struggle. The cost, in emotional turmoil, time and money, which led to my father's early death as a permanently embittered exile in a foreign country when he saw that after such sacrificial efforts the Negroes of Chicago were as ghetto-locked as ever, does not seem to figure in their calculations.

That is the reality that I am faced with when I now read that some Negroes my own age and younger say that we must now lie down in the streets, tie up traffic, do whatever we can —take to the hills with guns if necessary—and fight back. Fatuous people remark these days on our "bitterness." Why, of course we are bitter. The entire situation suggests that the nation be reminded of the too little noted final lines of Langston Hughes' mighty poem:

> What happens to a dream deferred?
> Does it dry up
> Like a raisin in the sun?
> Or fester like a sore—
> And then run?
> Does it stink like rotten meat?
> Or crust and sugar over—
> Like a syrupy sweet?
>
> Maybe it just sags
> Like a heavy load.
>
> *Or does it explode?*

Sincerely,

Lorraine Hansberry

II ❖

Sarah, I Kin Read

" This is the road from Jackson to Yazoo City, leading into the Mississippi Delta country, the heart of the Deep South... "

1.

My mother first took us south to visit her Tennessee birthplace one summer when I was seven or eight. I woke up on the back seat of the car while we were still driving through some place called Kentucky and my mother was pointing out to the beautiful hills and telling my brothers about how her father had run away and hidden from his master in those very hills when he was a little boy. She said that his mother had wandered among the wooded slopes in the moonlight and left food for him in secret places. They were very beautiful hills and I looked out at them for miles and miles after that wondering who and what a "master" might be.

I remember being startled when I first saw my grandmother rocking away on her porch. All my life I had heard that she was a great beauty and no one had ever remarked that they meant a half century before! The woman that I met was as wrinkled as a prune and could hardly hear and barely see and always seemed to be thinking of other times. But she could still rock and talk and even make wonderful cupcakes which were like cornbread, only sweet. She was captivated by automobiles and, even though it was well into the Thirties, I don't think she had ever been in one before we came down and took her driving. She was a little afraid and could not seem to negotiate the windows, but she loved driving.

She died the next summer and that is all that I remember about her, except that she was born in slavery and had memories of it and they didn't sound anything like *Gone With The Wind*. . . .

2.

LIGHTING *suggests a moonlit grove.* SARAH *emerges from the woods stealthily, searching. She is a young girl of nineteen.*

SARAH
(*Whispering*)
Hannibal. . . . Hannibal. . . .
(*She halts with a sigh of exasperation when her eyes see what they are looking for.* HANNIBAL *is lying with both arms folded under his head, staring up at the stars. He is a lean, vital young man with bright, commanding eyes. He smiles*)

25

HANNIBAL
(*Romantically—playing the poet-fool*)
And when she come to me, it were the moonrise. . . .
(*He holds out his hand playfully, himself
mocking the spirit of the mood he was en-
joying before* SARAH *appeared*)
And when she touch my hand, it were the true stars fallin'.
(*He takes her hand and pulls her down in
the grass and kisses her. She pulls away with
urgency*)

SARAH
Hannibal, what you always runnin' off for all the time? You
gonna catch you another whippin', boy.

HANNIBAL
Don't run off *all* the time . . .

SARAH
Oh, Hannibal!

HANNIBAL
(*Smiling, as he pulls a book out of his shirt*)
"Oh, Hannibal. Oh, Hannibal!"

SARAH
What you got there? . . .
(*As she recognizes the book with shock*)
Hannibal . . . Marster find you stole that Bible you be in
trouble bad!

HANNIBAL
(*In a mood to ignore peril*)
Me and you was *born* in trouble with Marster.

SARAH
What you think the Lord think of somebody who would steal
the holy book itself?

HANNIBAL
(*Smiling*)
What you think I would do with a Bible, Sarah?

26

(She clearly indicates she hasn't the vaguest notion. He waits—then)

Sarah, I kin read it.

(SARAH lifts her head slowly and just looks at him)

I kin. I kin read, Sarah.

(SARAH is speechless as he opens the Bible)

Listen—

(Placing one finger on the page and reading painfully because of the light and the newness of the ability)

"The—Book of—Jeremiah."

(He halts and looks in her face for the wonder which is waiting there)

SARAH
(Softly, with incredulity)

Hannibal—

(Then, suspiciously)

You can't make them marks out for real. You done memorized from prayer meetin'.

HANNIBAL
(Laughing gently)

No, Sarah—"And I said, O, that I had wings like a dove, then would I fly away and be at rest. . . ."

(He closes the book and looks at her. She stares at him in joy and wonder)

SARAH

That's where you go all the time—somebody been learnin' you—

(With sudden fear)

Don't you know what they do to you if they finds out?

HANNIBAL

Ain't nobody goin' to find out—don't you worry, little Sarah—

(Playfully switching to distract her from concern)

Hey, looka there—

27

SARAH
(*Noting him and also looking up*)

What—

HANNIBAL

Lookit that big, old, fat star shining away up yonder there!

SARAH
(*Automatically dropping her voice and looking about a bit*)

Shhh. Hannibal!

HANNIBAL
(*With his hand, as though he is personally touching the stars*)

1, 2, 3, 4—they makes up the dipper. That's the Big Dipper, Sarah. The ol' Drinkin' Gourd herself pointin' straight to the North Star! Sure is bright tonight. Sure would make good travelin' light tonight . . .

SARAH
(*With terror, clapping her hand over his mouth*)

Stop it! Trees on this plantation got more ears than leaves!

HANNIBAL
(*Moving her hand*)

—up there jes pointin' away—*due North!*

SARAH
(*Regarding him sadly*)

You're sure like your brother, boy. Just like him.

(HANNIBAL *ignores her and leans back. He sings softly to himself*)

HANNIBAL

"For the old man is a-waitin'
For to carry you to freedom
If you follow the drinking gourd.
Follow—follow—follow—
If you follow the drinking gourd . . ."

28

SARAH
(*Over the song*)
—look like him; talk like him; and God knows, you sure think
like him.
(*Pause*)
In time, I reckon—
(*Very sadly*)
—You be gone like him.

HANNIBAL
(*Sitting bolt upright suddenly and peering
into the woods about them*)
You think Isaiah got all the way to Canada, Sarah?
(*This last with true wonder*)
Sure he did! I bet you old Isaiah is up there and got hisself
a job and is livin' fine. I bet you that! Bet he works in a
lumber yard or something and got hisself a wife and maybe
even a house and—

SARAH
(*Quietly*)
You mean if he's alive, Hannibal.

HANNIBAL
Oh, he's alive all right!
(*He waits. Then, having assured himself
within*)
He's alive. And he's free.
(*He looks to the woods, remembering*)
I met him here that night to bring the food and a extry pair
of shoes. He was standing right over there, right over there,
with the moonlight streamin' down on him and he was
breathin' hard, Lord, that boy was breathin' so's you could
almost hear him on the other side of the woods.
(*A sudden pause and then a rush in the
telling*)
He didn't say nothing to me, nothin' at all. I jes hand him the
parcel and he put it in his shirt and give me a kind of push
on the shoulder.
(*He touches the place, remembering keenly*)
Here—. And then he turned and lit out through them woods
like lightnin'. He was bound out this place!

29

(*He is entirely quiet behind the completion of the narrative.* SARAH *is deeply affected by the implications of what she has heard and suddenly puts her arms around his neck and clings very tightly to him. Then she holds him back from her and looks at him for the truth*)

SARAH

You aim to go, don't you, Hannibal?
(*He does not answer and it is clear because of it that he intends to run off*)
H'you know it's so much better to run off?
(*A little desperately, near tears, thinking of the terrors involved*)
Even if you make it—h'you know what's up there, what it be like to go wanderin' round by yourself in this world?

HANNIBAL

I don't know. Jes know what it is to be a slave.

SARAH

We all slaves, Hannibal, but there's some as ain't got it so bad, who knows how to bend a little . . .

HANNIBAL

Then let'm bend. Me? I am the only kind of slave I could stand to be—a bad one. Every day that come and hour that pass that I got sense to make a half step do for a whole; every day that I can pretend sickness 'stead of health; to be stupid 'stead of smart, lazy 'stead of quick—I aims to do it. And the more pain it give Marster and the more it cost him —the more Hannibal be a *man!*

SARAH

Where would you go—?

HANNIBAL

Jes North, that's all I know.
(*Kind of shrugging*)
Try to find Isaiah maybe. How I know what I do?
(*Throwing up his hands at the difficult question*)

There's people up there what helps runaways.

> SARAH

You mean them aba—aba-litchinists? I heard Marster Sweet say
once that they catches runaways and makes soap out of
them.

> HANNIBAL
> (*Suddenly older and wiser*)

Oh, that's slave-owner talk, Sarah. Whatever you hear Marster
say 'bout slavery—you always believe the opposite . . .
Way I look at it, ever' slave ought to run off 'fore he die.

> SARAH
> (*Looking up suddenly absorbing the sense
> of what he has just said*)

Oh, Hannibal—*I* couldn't go!

> (*She starts to shake all over*)

I'm too delicate. My breath wouldn't hold out from here to
the river . . .

> HANNIBAL
> (*Starting to laugh at her*)

No, not you—skeerified as you is.

> (*He looks at her and pulls her to him*)

But don't you worry, little Sarah. I'll come back.

> (*He smooths her hair and comforts her*)

I'll come back and buy you. Mama too, if she's still livin'.

> (*The GIRL quivers in his arms and he holds
> her, looking up once again at the stars*)

I surely do that thing!

> THEY *freeze, dim slightly.* LIGHT
> UP *on* ZEB DUDLEY—*as before.*

> ZEB

You think God made these hands to sit idle while a man
watches his babies turn the color of death? . . . *I'M A
WHITE MAN, PREACHER!* And I'm going to drive
slaves for Everett Sweet if I have to and he's gonna pay me
for it and this time next year Zeb Dudley aims to own
himself some slaves and be a man, you hear!

31

III ⬦

White Fur in the
Middle of the
Depression

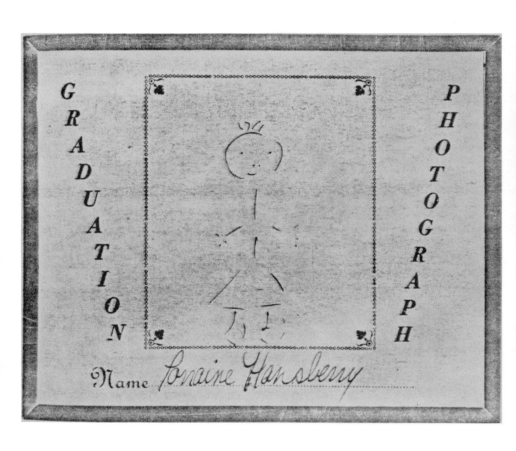

GRADUATION

PHOTOGRAPH

Name Lorraine Hansberry

1.

MY FAVORITE

Book: "River George" "Strange Fruit"

Songs: Black Magic and the Kerry Dance, Pomp and Circumstance

Game: Truth or Consequences

Heroes: Toussaint L'Ouverture and Hannibal

Chums: Erelene Ray, Lucille Robinson

Author: Pearl Buck

College: Wisconsin—Howard

High School: Englewood

Profession: Commercial Art and Law

Motto: United we stand, divided we fall.

2.

R–O–S–S
This spells Ross
We'll get along at any old cost
With one good Principal
& teachers all so fine
You may search the wide world over
No school like Ross you'll find.

The heartbreaking part was this: It was *not* an old building but, on the contrary, a relatively new and modern one. Its substandard quality had been planned from the drawing board. For from its inception Betsy Ross had been earmarked as a ghetto school, a school for black children and, therefore, one in which as many things as possible might be safely thought of as "expendable." That, after all, was why it existed: *not* to give education but to withhold as much as possible, just as the ghetto itself exists not to give people homes but to cheat them out of as much decent housing as possible.

I was given, during the grade school years, one-half the amount of education prescribed by the Board of Education of my city.

35

This was so because the children of the Chicago ghetto were jammed into a segregated school system. I am a product of that system and one result is that—to this day—I cannot count properly. I do not add, subtract or multiply with ease. Our teachers, devoted and indifferent alike, had to sacrifice something to make the system work at all—and in my case it was arithmetic that got put aside most often. Thus, the mind which was able to grasp university level reading materials in the sixth and seventh grades had not been sufficiently exposed to elementary arithmetic to make even simple change in a grocery store.

This is what is meant when we speak of the scars, the marks that the ghettoized child carries through life. To be imprisoned in the ghetto is to be forgotten—or deliberately cheated of one's birthright —at best.

3.

I recall being the only child in my classes who did not come from the Rooseveltian atmosphere of the homes of the Thirties. Father ran for Congress as a Republican. He believed in American private enterprise and, among other things which he had done by the time I was old enough to be aware of him, amassed—in the terms of his community—a "fortune," (though actually he had done absolutely nothing of the kind: relative to American society of the Nineteen Thirties and Forties Carl A. Hansberry had simply become a reasonably successful businessman of the middle class). But we are all shaped, are we not, by that particular rim of the soup-bowl where we swim, and I have remained throughout the balance of my life a creature formed in a community atmosphere where I was known as—a "rich" girl.

In any case, my mother sent me to kindergarten in white fur in the middle of the depression; the kids beat me up; and I think it was from that moment I became—a rebel. . . .

4.

Because it was the largest, most finely wrapped of all the boxes, she had noticed it for days. And when, at last, the morning came

36

and she was allowed to rip asunder the smooth white tissue paper and see what lay inside, the child could do nothing but sit stunned.

The grown-ups ohhhed and ahhhed around her.

They congratulated the mother.

They insisted that the outfit be put, at once, upon the child.

They touched the fur and exclaimed afresh with passion.

And all the while the child sat half ill with the outrage that had been committed against her Christmas. She was compelled to stand up, a small angry mannequin in her pajamas, while the coat was first lovingly shaken and then thrust upon her frame and buttoned to her chin quite as if she was about to go out into the cold. Then the muff was placed on her fists, and the scratching little cap on her brow.

Now she was ready and she was made to walk up and down so that the grown-ups could ooh and ahh yet another chorus. At the hall mirror she saw herself and the image in the long panel was even more awful than the imagined one: she looked exactly like one of the enormous stupid rabbits in her silly coloring books. She *hated* those rabbits. Several tears, fat and lush, rose at once and spilled down her cheeks and past her tight lips until they dripped directly onto the ermine. . . .

5.

But the oohs and aahs prevailed. Swathed in white she was sent to school where the children of the ghetto had promptly set upon her with fist and inkwell, and ever since then she had been antagonistic to the symbols of affluence. In fact, after that day she had chosen her friends with intense fascination from among—her assailants.

Children such as Carmen Smith, who invariably lived in walk-up flats where it was very bare and rugless and one was permitted to eat good-doing bologna sandwiches on white bread with mustard and hold them in the hands so that the bread got moist like cereal while Carmen, with her teensie plaits carefully parted off all over her head, talked to her mother, who lay on a mattress on the floor, with no spring or linen, looking very tired or sick, and who had to tell the girls about the chores that they would have to do when they came home from school because she would be gone to work by then. Children who, above all, had their own door keys: gleaming yellow metal, hung proudly, in her eyes, on a string around the neck! Throughout her childhood she had tried various props in fiercely jealous emulation: her skate key, stray keys found in the streets, any number of things, but make-believe wasn't the same.

Kids like Carmen Smith did more things and laughed harder when they laughed and they got to go to the movies alone on Saturday afternoons without adults and they knew all the secret things that grown-ups did and the secret words to describe them. They had authority and they were loud and bucked their eyes and cursed when their games went badly. *They were like grown-ups*— and she had admired them mightily.

6.

Above all, there had been an aspect of the society of kids from the ghetto which demanded utmost respect: *they* fought. The girls as well as the boys. THEY FOUGHT. If you were not right with them, or sometimes even if you were, there they were of an afternoon after school, standing waiting for you in the sunshine: a little gang of them in their gym shoes, milling close together, blocking off the sidewalk, daring you to break for it and try to run to the other side of the street where, if luck prevailed, one might gain the protection of some chance passing adult. That, ultimately, was the worst thing of all to do because they always got you after that. *Always.* It was better to continue on right into their midst, feigning the courage or at least nonchalance. Once into the center and face to face with the toughest—the others closing in around you, chanting whatever it was that they were chanting on that particular day—the dialogue began:

"She say you say that I wear dirty underwear."

"I didn't say that."

"Who you callin' a lie?"

"Calling nobody a lie."

"Yes, you are. You say you didn't say what I said you said!"

"I didn't."

A roar of indictment: "See—she just said it again! Hit her!"

Dreadful things generally ensued after that: a sudden blow by fist or palm or one's entire person seized in a hostile embrace of fury and thrown to the sidewalk, where the pebbly texture of the concrete cut into the elbows and the knees. But, above all, the sheer terror of it all—of the fact of violence. . . .

38

GIN BRIGGS

7.

The world in fact is divided in half as it is lived by me. There are those who think me the liveliest of types: a chattering, guitar-playing, slow-drag dancing, guzzling figure of renaissance well-being. And, still, there are the others, those latter-day images of the children of my youth who found me curious then—and still do. A serious odd-talking kid who could neither jump double dutch nor understand their games, but who—classically—envied them. And their costumes. And the things that, somehow, gave them joy: quarters, fights, and their fascination to come into the carpeted quiet of our apartment.

They, understandably, never understood (or believed) my envy —and they never will.

IV ⧫

Queen of the Ethiopes!

The Book of

A Review of a Year,
January, 1947, to January, 1948.

ENGLEWOOD HIGH SCHOOL
CHICAGO, ILLINOIS

LORRAINE VIVIAN HANSBERRY
President, Forum
Gym secretary
To be a journalist

1.

My High School Yearbook bears the dedication: "Englewood High trains for citizenship in a world of many different peoples. Who could better appreciate this wonderful country than our forefathers who traveled hundreds of miles from every known nation, seeking a land of freedom from discrimination of race, color or creed." And in illustration, there is this:

> *The Great Branches of Man at Englewood High:* in front, Mangolia Ali of East Indian Mohammedan descent; second couple, Nancy Diagre and Harold Bradley, Negroid; middle couple, Rosalind Sherr and William Krugman, Jewish religion, not a racial stock; next, Eleanor Trester and Theodore Flood, Caucasoid; extreme right, Lois Lee and Barbara Nomura, Mongoloid; rear, left, Mr. Thompson, principal.

2.

I was reminded of Englewood by a questionnaire which came from *Show* magazine the other day. . . .

THE SHAKESPEAREAN EXPERIENCE
SHOW POLL #5, February 1964

Some Questions Answered by: Robert Bolt, Jean Cocteau, T. S. Eliot, Tyrone Guthrie, Lorraine Hansberry, Joan Littlewood, Harold Pinter, Alain Robbe-Grillet, Igor Stravinsky, Harry S Truman

QUESTION: *What was your first contact with Shakespeare?*

High School. English literature classwork. We had to read and memorize speeches from *Macbeth* and *Julius Caesar* all under the auspices of a strange and bewigged teacher who we, after this induction, naturally and cruelly christened "Pale Hecate"—God rest her gentle, enraptured and igniting soul!

> PALE HECATE *enters, ruler in hand, and takes her place in the class-room.* SHE *surveys the* CLASS. THEY *come to attention as her eye falls on* EACH *in turn.*

43

PALE HECATE

Y'do not read, nor speak, nor write the English language! I suspect that y'do not even *think* in it! God only knows in what language y'do think, or if you think at all. 'Tis true the *English* have done little enough with the tongue, but being the English I expect it was the best they could do.

(*They giggle*)

In any case, I'll have it learned properly before a living one of y'll pass out of this class. That I will!

(*Waving a composition book and indicating the grade marked in red at the top*)

As for *you*, Miss—as for you, indeed, surely you will recognize the third letter of the alphabet when y'have seen it?

STUDENT

"C."

PALE HECATE

Aye, a "C" it 'tis! You're a bright and clever one now after all, aren't y'lass?

(*The class snickers*)

And now, my brilliance, would you also be informing us as to what a grade signifies when it is thus put upon the page?

STUDENT

Average.

PALE HECATE

"Average." Yes, yes—and what else in your case, my iridescence? Well then, I'll be tellin' you in fine order. It stands for "cheat," my luminous one!

(*The class sobers*)

For them that will do *half* when *all* is called for; for them that will slip and slide through life at the edge of their minds, never once pushing into the interior to see what wonders are hiding there—content to drift along on whatever gets them by, *cheating* themselves, *cheating* the world, *cheating* Nature! That is what the "C" means, my dear child—

(*She smiles*)

—my pet

(*They giggle; in rapid order she raps each on the head with her ruler*)

—my laziest *Queen of the Ethiopes!*

SHE *exists or dims out.*

44

QUESTION: *Which is your favorite Shakespeare play and why?*

Favorite? It is like choosing the "superiority" of autumn days; mingling titles permits a reply: *Othello* and *Hamlet*. Why? There is a sweetness in the former that lingers long after the tragedy is done. A kind of possibility that we suspect in man wherein even its flaw is a tribute. The latter because there remains a depth in the Prince that, as we all know, constantly re-engages as we mature. And it does seem that the wit remains the brightest and most instructive in all dramatic literature.

QUESTION: *What is the most important result of your familiarity with Shakespeare? What has he given you?*

Comfort and agitation so bound together that they are inseparable. Man, as set down in the plays, is large. Enormous. Capable of anything at all. And yet fragile, too, this view of the human spirit; one feels it ought be respected and protected and loved rather fiercely.

Rollicking times, Shakespeare has given me. I love to laugh and his humor is that of everyday; of every man's foible at no man's expense. Language. At 13 a difficult and alien tedium, those Elizabethan cadences; but soon a balm, a thrilling source of contact with life. . . .

3.

But Shakespeare notwithstanding, neither "Pale Hecate" nor Mr. Thompson ("rear, left, principal") could do much with the Great Branches of Man at Englewood High—"Negroid, Mongoloid, Caucasoid" *or* "Jewish"—on the day of the race riot and strike at school.

Oh, yes, she remembered! She remembered, and would never forget, how, on that day, the well-dressed colored students like herself had stood amusedly around the parapet, staring, simply staring at the mob of several hundred striking whites, trading taunts and insults—but showing not the least inclination to further assert racial pride.

Then had come the veterans—volunteers from Wendell Phillips High School and DuSable, carloads of them, waving baseball bats and shouting slogans of the charge. The word had gone into the ghetto: *The ofays are out on strike and beating up and raping colored girls under the viaduct out South!* And the summary, traditional and terse: WE BETTER GO 'CAUSE THEM LITTLE CHICKEN-SHIT NIGGERS OUT THERE AIN'T *ABOUT* TO FIGHT!

And so they had come, pouring out of the bowels of the ghetto, the children of the unqualified oppressed: the black workingclass in their costumes of pegged pants and conked heads and tight skirts and almost knee-length sweaters and—worst of all—*colored* anklets, held up by rubber bands!

Yes, they had come and they had fought. It had taken the Mayor and the visit of a famous movie star to get everyone's mind back on other things again. He had been terribly handsome and full of speeches on "tolerance" and had also given a lot of autographs. But she had been unimpressed.

She never could forget one thing: *They had fought back!*

V

WISCONSIN:
Of Vikings and
Congo Drums

1.

Only the snow could have coaxed Candace from the warmth of the fire and the crossword puzzle. The glorious, cold, clean Wisconsin snow—certainly not classes! To hell with Life Drawing 101 and Fine Arts 3: Breughel would have chosen these hills, the black trees of winter, the friendly but somber evergreens—and the snow.

She stood now just below the great arch of the ski jump on the high slope above the Student Union building: she stood with her arms wrapped around her looking down at the lake. A few early skaters moved in dark silhouettes against the blue white of the ice. She watched them and thought of primeval things. Men and ice? When had they first found that they could put runners on their feet and master even rivers! She had read Thoreau the year before and the passages on skating had stuck.

Beyond, across the lake, mounted on the white hills, were the trees. She had come to this very spot to salute them her first winter here; autumns she came and watched them fling their gifts to the ground. Softly, huge white flakes began to fall. She sighed. The snow was about the only thing that had not disappointed her in two years of college. The cold clean drifts of Wisconsin snow. In every other way college was a bust.

2.

She had begun her college career awkwardly and it had stayed that way. The point of things eluded her—things like classes and note-taking and lecture and lab. She found most of them unspeakably dull and irrelevant to virtually anything she had ever had on her mind or ever expected to. Worst of all was something called "Physical Geography," which required, among other things, that she spend some four hours a week knocking on rocks with a little metal hammer; she had been so out of what it was all about when she signed up that she had actually thought she was enlisting in a course in ordinary social geography. She had flunked it square.

And most things had gone something like that.

She did not, of course, flunk *everything*. An average of something had to be maintained just to stay there, and she maintained that through the balancing out of the literature, art, history and philosophy courses—but only *just*—waiting at the end of each semester for the least fraction of points to be tallied up to see whether she was in or out.

All that she had imagined college to be had yet to materialize. The only thing which had not disappointed was—the snow. What, what was it about the snow?

3.

Was the European part of her bloodstream Viking perhaps? She didn't really *believe* in "blood" feelings. Still this affinity for austere winter . . . ? The slave-masters—great-grandfathers of hers on both sides who had forced themselves upon her slave great-grandmothers—who were they? Candace knew only that she was of that composition that defined many, if not indeed most American Negroes: the continents of the world met in her blood—Africa, Europe and aboriginal America. Still, one did not hear of *Viking* slaveowners particularly. . . .

English then? Her mental association with the types from the British Isles who had mainly owned her ancestors and in part begot her was a fairly traditional one, automatically conjuring up thin-faced, thin-blooded, watery-eyed decadents in riding boots, pawing noble black women in ripped muslin with faces turned away in silent, helpless outrage.

But Vikings—that was something else. Scandinavian lore had once captivated her; indeed she had been obsessed with images of tall grunting blonde folk in fur capes and horns and belted leggings moving through dark forests grunting Beowulf and building funny churches with turned-up edges and having sex in hay lofts. . . . Where, where did these images come from? It was true that she had read *Kristin Lavransdatter* in her high-school years—but the great trilogy had only deepened notions that had already been there. In any case she thought it was all very beautiful, blue snow and pale yellow-haired people grunting around. . . .

As for the African part, the greater part, she had spent hours of her younger years poring over maps of the African continent, postulating and fantasizing: *Ibo, Mandingo, Hausa, Yoruba, Ashanti, Dahomean.* Who, who were they! In her emotions she was sprung from the Southern Zulu and the Central Pygmy, the Eastern Watusi and the treacherous slave-trading Western Ashanti themselves. She was Kikuyu and Masai, ancient cousins of hers had made the exquisite forged sculpture at Benin, while surely even more ancient relatives sat upon the throne at Abu Simbel watching over the Nile.

50

One thing was certain: she was at one, texture, blood, follicles of hair, nerve ends, all with the sound of a mighty Congo drum. She had never heard African music that had not set her mad with the romance of her people, *never*. At the first rich basso boom, her heart rose in her bosom, her teeth set, her eyes widened, and Africa claimed her. . . .

4.

And there she stood now in the snow, thinking perhaps that the poles of the earth had met in her . . . until she realized suddenly that she was not alone on the slope. He was wearing a neat, thin, and distinctly uncampus coat—and *he* was not a Viking.

> DIM UP *on* CANDACE *and on* MO-NASSE, *an African student, standing, shivering, some distance from her.*

CANDACE
(*Laughing and approaching him*)
If you are that cold, why on earth stand out here?

MONASSE
(*With definite African accent*)
It is cold everywhere in your country. At least, here it is beautiful.

CANDACE
(*Eyes lighting with recognition*)
It is cold everywhere *out of doors* in my country. We do have steam heat.

MONASSE
(*Quite taken with her*)
I am willing to go in if you will have tea with me.

51

CANDACE

Tea . . . !

Tea, she thought—and the *accent!* She thought of Casablanca
and intrigue and Ingrid Bergman and black men peering out from
white blankets in the desert. She would try his tea. . . .

(MONASSE *and* CANDACE *cross and sit*)

MONASSE

NEZ-AH—

CANDACE
(*Imitatively*)

NEZ-AH—

MONASSE

NETT—

CANDACE

NETT

MONASSE

AH-HOON!

CANDACE

AH-HOON!

MONASSE

There, you have it! *Netsanett ahun!* Freedom now.

CANDACE

Netsanett ahun!

MONASSE

Wonderful.

CANDACE
(*Showing off and stumbling only slightly*)

Indemin—Newo.

52

MONASSE
You should major in languages instead of art.

CANDACE
Selam.

(They laugh)
Sing the anthem for me again, Monasse.

MONASSE
(Declining)
Oh, please—

CANDACE
No, please, sing it—I love the way you say, É-tee-ope-ia!

MONASSE
Very well.
(Imitating her)
E-tee-ope-ia.

CANDACE
(After a moment, eagerly)
What are we going to do about South Africa?
(He looks at her, puzzled)
There are South African students here. White, of course. We
don't speak to them.

MONASSE
"We"?

CANDACE
Well, *I* don't.

MONASSE
Do they speak to *you?*

CANDACE
Well, now, that's not the point, is it? I'd just as soon smack
one of them in the teeth as not. Hate them.
(He roars)

And you—don't *you* care?
                    (*Suddenly suspicious*)
Or are you a prince or something?

                    MONASSE
I am not, I assure you, a prince.

                    CANDACE
Well, *what* are you? I know that there aren't too many poor
    Ethiopians running around over here.

                    MONASSE
I didn't say that I was poor. I said that I was not a prince.

                    CANDACE
                    (*Accusingly*)
A colonial bourgeois then.

                    MONASSE
I am descended from merchants, yes.

                    CANDACE
I thought so!

                    MONASSE
But Ethiopia is not a colony—

                    CANDACE
Economically it is!

                    MONASSE
I see.

                    CANDACE
Well, don't you *care*—

                    MONASSE
About what, my dear?

CANDACE

About Africa! The liberation!

MONASSE

You are unbelieveable. I cannot wait for Assan to see what I
have found.

CANDACE

I am not a "what"!

(*Afterthought*)

Assan?

MONASSE

My countryman—

(*As her eyes light*)

You will have to ask him yourself if *he* "cares" about the
liberation.

(*She turns away, hurt*)

What is the matter?

CANDACE

(*Sulking*)

Why are you making fun of me?

MONASSE

Because you delight me.

CANDACE

I do? How?

MONASSE

(*Smiling*)

What do they do to the children in this country that one must
constantly compliment people in order to have a conversation.

CANDACE

(*After a moment*)

Were you in the resistance?

MONASSE

What resistance?

CANDACE

Against the Italians.

MONASSE

I was four years old then; my cell was never called into action.

CANDACE
(*Flushed*)

Oh, of course. It doesn't seem that long ago. I remember the newsreels as if it were yesterday. You fought tanks with spears. I must have been only four or five myself, but I remember crying. And the Pope—when he blessed the Italian soldiers my mother told us never to forget what Catholicism stood for!
(*Mock spitting gesture*)

MONASSE

Don't do that.

CANDACE

Why?

MONASSE

It is unladylike.

CANDACE

"Unladylike." My God, you are feudalistic, aren't you!
(*Pause*)
Is it true that they threw virgins into shark tanks during the occupation?

MONASSE

"Virgins"? They threw *people* in shark tanks.

CANDACE
(*Wistfully*)

I wish I were an African . . .

56

MONASSE
(*Nodding*)
So you could be—a revolutionary?

CANDACE
Millions of Africans marching, singing, carrying their leaders
on their shoulders—

MONASSE
You've seen only thousands at the most so far; and the shoulders of other men is not a very good place for leaders. . . .

CANDACE
Why are you always like that?

MONASSE
Like what?

CANDACE
Well, so disparaging about all the *big* things.

MONASSE
(*Meeting her eyes intently*)
Because you are serious enough about them for both of us,
I think.
THEY *freeze.*

Six "serious" hours later she arrived back at the dorm filled to
bursting and savouring every detail she would have for Mariela.
She was sure of it now: he hadn't *said* it but the look was unmistakable in his eyes: *Monasse had his ties with the Liberation!* And,
moreover, right in the middle of page 238 of *Facing Mt. Kenya*,
he had closed the book and kissed her. That ought to hold good ole'
Mariela!

LIGHTS UP *on* MARIELA, *manicur-
ing her toenails with marked con-
centration.* CANDACE *enters breath-
lessly.*

57

CANDACE

Mariela—

(*She is immediately waved to silence while* MARIELA *completes a critical part of the process. At last—*)

Listen, have I got news!

MARIELA
(*Perfunctory nod*)

Mmmnn.

(*Then, deadpan*)

Kitten, I'm pregnant.

CANDACE
(*Long silence*)

My God, you've been *sleeping* with him!

MARIELA

Well, there are no new stars in the heavens, are there!

CANDACE
(*Open-mouthed*)

Well—Well—

(*She sinks into a chair and they stare at each other*)

Well, boy, that's what I hate about these intellectual type friendships. Doesn't he *wear* anything? Don't *you?* Mariela —you'll have to have an abortion and all that. How grisly!

MARIELA

Nope, not going to have it. Want the baby.

CANDACE

You do?

MARIELA

Yes I do. That's why I didn't "use" anything as you put it. I wanted it to happen.

CANDACE

You did?

58

MARIELA

I did. And I do. Listen, Can—I am very, very happy. I think
Karl is too.

(*Her eyes cloud over just the least little bit*)

I *think* he is. . . .

(*Brightening*)

And if it works out—we'll get married.

CANDACE

And if it doesn't?

MARIELA

We won't.

CANDACE

But Mariela, what are you going to *do* with it? Take it to class
every day?

MARIELA

(*Teacher to slow pupil*)

I'm going to quit, stupid. I've found what I wanted in college.
For the rest—I can read.

> SHE *exits grandly with* CANDACE
> *at her heels—who almost immedi-
> ately returns with* MONASSE. BOTH
> *are carrying books.* SHE *stops sud-
> denly and faces him:*

CANDACE

(*Outraged*)

What in the name of God are you talking about? Mariela is
my friend. A perfectly marvelous girl—

MONASSE

Well, apparently a little free.

CANDACE

Oh, brother—

(*Wiggling her thumbs*)

—has Ethiopia got a long way to go!

MONASSE
(*A little surprised*)
Then you really think her behavior is acceptable for—a decent young woman?

CANDACE
Her behavior? You think she got that way by just letting him stare at her or something!

MONASSE
Well, of course, he's responsible. But one only presumes in the first place with certain kinds of girls—

CANDACE
(*In genuine astonishment*)
Why, you really are medieval. I bet you believe in harems!

MONASSE
(*Without humor*)
I do not. That is slavery and I do not find slavery acceptable in any form.

CANDACE
Just the old North African version of the double standard, hey? "The boys can and the girls can't."
(*Loftily—raising the banner. He looks about with embarrassment*)
Long live the Industrial Revolution! Long live the United States! Long live—the Kinsey Report!

MONASSE
Well, now . . . society has to make some rules to protect itself . . . to protect children . . .

CANDACE
Listen, haven't you ever heard of contraceptives?
(*He is dumbfounded*)
Well, what do you think they are for!

60

MONASSE
(*An effort at dignity*)
I haven't the least intention of discussing this matter with a young woman I respect.

CANDACE
And you call yourself a revolutionary!
(*He opens his mouth to speak—hesitates—looks in vain for the referee*)
Well, I'll bet you at least one-half of the girls on this campus have them—diaphragms—and use them! And it's growing all the time. And, well, when the pill comes in—well, *all* the excuses will be over then! Women will be exactly as free as men. Long live—

MONASSE
(*Holding up his hand for peace*)
I sincerely hope so.

CANDACE
(*She pauses, triumphant. Then, not quite yet ready to let go*)
And as for Mariela—my *friend* does it with the boy she loves and she doesn't do anything to prevent pregnancy because she WANTS the baby! It's all open and loving. *That* is decency . . .

MONASSE
Why—would you have done that if I had asked . . .

CANDACE
(*Open-mouthed*)
Well—well—
(*The victory march has become a rout*)
Well . . . not after *talking* about it like this and everything . . .

MONASSE
(*Gently*)
I'm sorry. I truly didn't mean to embarrass you. You were speaking about it so—clinically—that I forgot myself.

CANDACE

Sex does *not* embarrass me! I probably know more about it right now than your mother with all her children and everything!

MONASSE
(*A little stunned to find his mother in this particular conversation*)

I dare say.

(*He looks at her. They laugh. Suddenly she freezes.*)

CANDACE

Listen, were you just getting . . . information just now? I mean, when you asked me what you did? Or were you asking me to? I don't know with you. With an American boy it would have been a sneaky lead-up, you know?

MONASSE
(*Laughing*)

I was getting information. It would be—
(*He hesitates and smiles*)
—against my principles to sleep with you under the present circumstances.

CANDACE
(*Relieved—and disappointed*)

Oh.

MONASSE

Mind you, I said *my* principles. Do not take it in your head that *every* Ethiopian would therefore feel the same!
THEY *freeze.*

She had not planned it earlier, but now she made up her mind. On behalf of American women—and world emancipation—she would change his mind about a number of things. "Nice girls" and "bad girls" belonged in the Middle Ages and she was going to bring one gorgeous black knight-without-armor into the twentieth century!

VI ✧

Take Away Our Hearts O' Stone

1.

LIGHT UP *on* JUNO BOYLE *in a moment from Sean O'Casey's* Juno and the Paycock.

JUNO

Oh Blessed Virgin, where were you when me darlin' son was riddled with bullets—when me darlin' son was riddled with bullets! . . . *Sacred heart of the Crucified Jesus, take away our hearts o' stone* . . . *an' give us hearts of flesh!* . . .

I remember rather clearly that my coming had been an accident. Also that I sat in the orchestra close to the stage: the orchestra of the great modern building which is the main theater plant of the University of Wisconsin. The woman's voice, the howl, the shriek of misery fitted to a wail of poetry that consumed all my senses and all my awareness of human pain, endurance and the futility of it—

JUNO

. . . *Take away this murdherin' hate* . . . *an' give us Thine own eternal love!*

Now Mrs. Madigan reappeared with her compassionate shawl and the wail rose and hummed through the tenement, through Dublin, through Ireland itself and then mingled with seas and became something born of the Irish wail that was all of us. I remember sitting there stunned with a melody that I thought might have been sung in a different meter. The play was *Juno*, the writer Sean O'Casey—but the melody was one that I had known for a very long while.

I was seventeen and I did not think then of *writing* the melody as *I* knew it—in a different key; but I believe it entered my consciousness and stayed there. . . .

2.

MUSIC—*a good loud Southside blues.* LIGHTS UP. RUTH YOUNGER *is ironing as* BENEATHA, *her teenage sister-in-law, enters grandly, draped in African robes.*

65

BENEATHA

You are looking at what a well-dressed Nigerian woman wears!

(RUTH's *mouth falls and she puts down the iron in fascination.* BENEATHA *parades, coquettishly fanning herself with an* LP *record* —*mistakenly more like Madame Butterfly than any Nigerian that ever was*—*then suddenly flicks off the radio with a flourish*)

Enough of this assimilationist junk!

(*She puts the record on, turns, waits ceremoniously*—*and abruptly leaps with a shout*)

OCOMOGOSIAY!!!

(RUTH *jumps. The* DRUMS *and* MUSIC *come up, a lovely Nigerian melody.* BENEATHA *listens, enraptured, her eyes far away.* SHE *begins to dance.* RUTH *is dumbfounded*)

RUTH

(*Drily, skeptically*—*and very idiomatically*)

What kind of dance is that?

BENEATHA

A folk dance.

RUTH

(*Pearl Bailey*)

What kind of folks do that, honey?

BENEATHA

It's from Nigeria. It's a dance of welcome.

RUTH

Who you welcoming?

BENEATHA

The men back to the village.

RUTH

Where they been?

BENEATHA

How should I know—out hunting or something. Anyway, they are coming back now . . .

RUTH

Well, that's good.

BENEATHA
(*Singing with the record*)

Alundi, alundi
Alundi alunya
Jop pu a jeepua
Ang gu sooooooooooo
Ai yai yae . . .
ayehaye—alundi.

> (WALTER *comes in during this performance;
he has obviously been drinking. He leans
against the door heavily and watches his
sister, at first with distaste. Then his eyes
look off—"back to the past"—as he lifts both
his fists to the roof screaming*)

WALTER

YEAH . . . AND ETHIOPIA STRETCH FORTH HER ARMS AGAIN! . . .

RUTH
(*Drily, looking at him*)

Yes—and Africa sure is claiming her own tonight.
> (*She gives them both up and starts ironing
again*)

WALTER
(*All in a drunken, dramatic shout*)

Shut up! . . . I'm digging them drums. . . .

> THEY *freeze but* LIGHT *holds and*
> DRUMS *continue lightly under*—
> LIGHT UP *on* O'Casey's JUNO
> BOYLE, *as before, responding to
> the offstage voice of her husband
> singing in deep, sonorous, inebri-
> ated tones.*

BOYLE

"*Sweet Spirit, hear me prayer! Hear . . . oh . . . hear
. . . me prayer . . . hear, oh, hear . . . Oh, he . . . ar
. . . oh, he . . . ar . . . me . . . pray . . . er!*" *Ah,
that's a darlin' song, a daaarlin' song!*

JUNO
(*Viciously, as he enters*)
*Sweet spirit hear his prayer! Ah, then, I'll take me solemn
affedavey, it's not for a job he's prayin'! . . .*

BOYLE
Are you never goin' to give us a rest?

JUNO
*Oh, you're never tired o'lookin' for a rest . . . If there was
e'er a genuine job goin' you'd be dh'other way about . . .
You'd do far more work with a knife and fork, me boyo,
than ever you'll do with a shovel! Your poor wife slavin'
to keep the bit in your mouth, an' you gallivantin' about
all the day like a paycock!*

BOYLE
D'ye want to dhrive me out o' the house?

JUNO
*It ud be easier to dhrive you out o' the house than to dhrive
you into a job!*

> THEY *freeze.* DRUMS UP *for a mo-
> ment, then under—the* RECORDED
> VOICE *of Lorraine Hansberry in
> the midst of an interview.* JUNO,
> BOYLE, WALTER, RUTH *and* BE-
> NEATHA *remain.*

L. H.

I love Sean O'Casey. This, to me, is the playwright of the
twentieth century accepting and using the most obvious instruments of Shakespeare, which is the human personality in
its totality. O'Casey never fools you about the Irish, you see
. . . the Irish drunkard, the Irish braggart, the Irish liar . . .
and the genuine heroism which must naturally emerge when

68

you tell the truth about people. This, to me, is the height of artistic perception and is the most rewarding kind of thing that can happen in drama, because when you believe people so completely—because *everybody* has their drunkards and their braggarts and their cowards, you know—then you also believe them in their moments of heroic assertion: you don't doubt them.

> JUNO *and* BOYLE *fade out.* DRUMS UP — WALTER-BENEATHA-RUTH *scene resumes.*

WALTER

. . . them drums move me!
> (*He makes his weaving way to his wife's face and leans in close*)
In my *heart of hearts*—
> (*He thumps his chest*)
—I am much warrior!

RUTH
> (*Without even looking up*)
In your heart of hearts you are much drunkard.

WALTER
> (*Starting to wander the room*)
Me and Jomo . . .
> (*Intently, in his sister's face. She has stopped dancing to watch him in this unknown mood*)
That's my man—Kenyatta.
> (*Shouting and thumping his chest*)
FLAMING SPEAR! HOT DAMN!
> (*He is suddenly in possession of an imaginary spear and actively spearing enemies all over the room*)
OCOMOGOSIAY . . . THE LION IS WAKING . . . OWIMOWEH!
> (*He pulls his shirt open and leaps up on a table*)

69

BENEATHA
(*To encourage* WALTER)
OCOMOGOSIAY, FLAMING SPEAR!

WALTER
(*On the table, very far gone, his eyes pure glass sheets. He sees what we cannot, that he is a leader of his people, a great chief, a descendant of Chaka, and that the hour to march has come*)
Listen, my black brothers—

BENEATHA
OCOMOGOSIAY!

WALTER
—Do you hear the waters rushing against the shores of the coastlands—

BENEATHA
OCOMOGOSIAY!

WALTER
(*And now the* LIGHTING *shifts subtly to suggest the world of* WALTER'*s imagination— and he assumes an unexpected majesty*)
—Do you hear the screeching of the cocks in yonder hills beyond where the chiefs meet in council for the coming of the mighty war—

BENEATHA
OCOMOGOSIAY!

WALTER
—Do you hear the beating of the wings of the birds flying low over the mountains and the low places of our land—
(*Doorbell rings.* RUTH *goes to answer*)

BENEATHA
OCOMOGOSIAY!

WALTER

—Do you hear the singing of the women, singing the war songs of our fathers to the babies in the great houses . . . singing the sweet war songs? *Oh, do you hear, my black brothers!*

BENEATHA
(*Completely gone*)

We hear you, Flaming Spear—

RUTH
(*Admitting* GEORGE MURCHISON, BENEATHA'S *well-dressed date*)

Come in, George—

WALTER

Telling us to prepare for the greatness of the time—
(*To* GEORGE, *extending his hand for the fraternal clasp*)

BLACK BROTHER!

GEORGE

Black Brother, hell! What is this—a *Mau Mau* meeting?!

3.

I shall never forget when Frank Lloyd Wright came and spoke at the University in the brand new and ever so modernistic Union Building Auditorium. There was a rustle and a stir on campus for days before—and finally there they were, he and his entourage *sweeping* in, it seems to me now, in capes and string ties and long hair.

Later, addressing the packed hall, he attacked almost everything —and, foremost among them, the building he was standing in for its violation of the organic principles of architecture; he attacked babbitry and the nature of education saying that we put in so many fine plums and get out so many fine prunes. Everyone laughed— the faculty nervously I guess; but the students cheered.

I left the University shortly after to pursue an education of another kind . . .

VII ⟨✦⟩

NEW YORK:
Baby,
You Could Be
Jesus in Drag...

Harlem church, a Baptist church. It's not a Sunday and nobody is dressed up. People out on the sidewalk in front of the church ask: who is it? And somebody with an angry face whispers the answer.

When you go in, it's quiet.

Nobody is crying.

It's just quiet.

And then we wait.

You think while you wait. The hymn board up over the pulpit says: Psalm number 13. The church reminds you of all the Sundays you have ever known. Soap and flower odors . . . and music. Most of all it reminds of music.

And you wait.

Somebody comes and says people are going to drive over and see what is wrong, what's holding things up, and will you go?

And you agree.

You get up and walk out to the car and you drive through the Harlem streets and then you sit in the car a few seconds waiting and the minister says someone should go in and ask and you say that you will. And you put your hand on the aluminum handle of the car and it seems heavy to move, but you finally open the door and you get out and walk toward the place and your feet seem heavy on the Harlem sidewalk, but after a few seconds you are there.

You go in and it is quiet here too, and dark.

Why haven't they come? you ask. What is wrong? We, the friends, the relatives, we are waiting at the church.

And the man says there has been a delay but they are coming now. And so you walk around the place, close to the long pastel boxes. There are two long ones and a very small one. And you wonder about the small one. And then you go up close to the long copper-colored one and look in it.

He was very big.

He was handsome and his face still looks kind.

You can't see his fists, they are under that part which is closed, but you get the feeling that they are balled up tight.

You stand watching him a long time. And an old woman comes and stands beside you and she asks you what was wrong with him, such a *strong* young man. You tell her he was killed, shot. The cops, she asks—did a cop do it? And you say, yes, it was a cop. And she shakes her head.

He is very *young*, she says. Where was he killed, she asks, and you tell her. And she looks at you and she looks at him. And she says she guesses it don't make no difference about going to school then.

And you are quiet.

2.

People say to me, what makes you so suspicious? Ha! In this world to think some even dare ask! I was twenty when I came to this city. Twenty. I met a boy then, girls do. He was twenty-three or something like that, I think, and he had already been married and already had a child but not divorced. It had not occurred to me that young men could already have wives and children when they came to call. He also had buddies and they wrote to him for narcotics while they were away. That was how I found out that he took heroin, sniffed it, they say. And I, who knew nothing of such things, found this out. And now it is impossible when people say to me: why are you so suspicious?

3.

New York City

Dear Edythe,

I was lying across the bed in my room and it was dark and hot and July and New York and 1951 and thinking about nothing in particular except that I was tired and very unsleepy . . . and then I thought of you, and now I am at my typewriter writing you.

I don't really know where you are and certainly not what kind of thoughts you think these days, and at this particular moment I don't care, but I was struck in those moments that I just described with a familiar old need: to chat a bit. And I think at this time we can be honest and admit that what we liked most about one another was our mutual ability to listen and read.

I am living in New York now, since last November, and I can't remember when I wrote you last or how much I told you when I did write. Probably a lot of nonsense about Greenwich Village. Fact is, I have finally stopped going to school and started working. Which means a lot of things. I work for the new Negro paper, FREEDOM, which in its time in history ought to be *the* journal of Negro liberation . . . in fact, it will be.

I live (to my total dissatisfaction) on the lower east side; share an apartment with three other girls. Very nice modern little four room job . . . would prefer to live in Harlem however, but it is too damn crowded in the ghetto for even those who want to move in . . . But something may happen. My roommates are nice. So is the place but there is little privacy and I am writing in a serious way these days.

Otherwise: you might want to know what I look like. I am considerably slimmer than you remember me, have stopped whacking my hair off and it's at some strange length, some of the blemishes have disappeared off my face and I think I smile less, but perhaps with more sincerity when I do. I work five days a week typing (eh?) receptionist and writer, and take home $31.70, which I think must account for the slimness. See only foreign movies, no plays hardly; have learned to love clothes in a new way . . . life in a new way. I think I am a little different. Attend meetings almost every night, sing in a chorus, eat all the foreign foods in New York, usher at rallies, make street corner speeches in Harlem, sometimes make it up to the country on Sundays, go for long walks in Harlem and talk to my people about everything on the streets. . . .

4.

LIGHT UP *on* FIRST BLACK WOMAN, *a young domestic worker.*

YOUNG WOMAN

All right. So now you know something 'bout me you didn't know! In these streets out there, any little white boy from Long Island or Westchester sees me and leans out of his car and yells—"Hey there, *hot chocolate!* Say there, Jezebel! Hey you—'Hundred Dollar Misunderstanding'! YOU! Bet you know where there's a good time tonight. . . ."

Follow me sometimes and see if I lie. I can be coming from eight hours on an assembly line or fourteen hours in Mrs. Halsey's kitchen. I can be all filled up that day with three hundred years of rage so that my eyes are flashing and my flesh is trembling—and the white boys in the streets, they look at me and think of sex. They look at me and that's *all* they think. . . . Baby, you could be Jesus in drag—but if you're brown they're sure you're selling!

5.

I suppose that the most heroic expression that I have ever seen was that on the face of a certain tough-looking, brutalized, slum-slaughtered woman at Coney Island. She had her arm around a girl child who looked hardly any less brutalized and slum-slaughtered— "*We is going to have a good time tonight!*" the look said.

6.

The editor wore a large black moustache in those days and he was seated in an office on Lenox Avenue behind a desk arranged in front of a large curving window that allowed one to see a lot of Harlem at one time. It seems to me now that there were few things in that office other than the desk, the two chairs we sat on, a lonely typewriter, some panels of gray afternoon light—and the altogether commanding personality of Louis E. Burnham.

His voice was very deep and his language struck my senses immediately with its profound literacy, constantly punctuated by deliberate and loving poetic lapses into the beloved color of the speech of the masses of our people. He invariably made his eyes very wide when he said things in idiom and, sometimes, in the middle of a story, he just opened his mouth and howled for the joy of it. I suppose it was because of his voice, so rich, so strong, so very certain, that I never associated fragility with Louis Burnham despite his slight frame.

The things he taught me were great things: that all racism was rotten, white or black, that *everything* is political; that people tend to be indescribably beautiful and uproariously funny. He also taught me that they have enemies who are grotesque and that freedom lies in the recognition of all of that and other things.

I had just turned twenty when I met him and I told him about the novel I had wanted to write when I was eighteen. I told him how I was desperately worried about having become too jaded, at twenty, to retain all the lovely things I had wanted to say in my novel when I was eighteen. It was part of his genius as a human being that he did not laugh at all or patronize my dilemma, but went on to gently and seriously prod me to consider the possibilities of the remaining time of my life.

I recall how he kept turning back and forth from that window that let him look at Harlem while he talked to me. The thing he had for our people was something marvelous; he gave part of it to me and I shall die with it as he did. He would say simply, "They are beautiful, child," and close his eyes sometimes. And I always knew that he could see them marching then.

It was an open and adoring love that mawkishness never touched. . . .

7.

LIGHT UP *on* SECOND BLACK
WOMAN, *a chic professional
woman of middle-age.*

OLDER WOMAN
"Hey there, *hot chocolate!* Say there, Jezebel! YOU! . . ."
The white boys in the streets, they look at *me* and think
of sex. They look at me and that's *all* they think!

8.

The point about segregation is: imagine the insult of a conversation to my face of *Florida*—where just in the last month the latest
(publicized) lynching has taken place. Florida. They speak of it
with warmth and love in my very face—
Bloody land of hatreds!

9.

FOR A YOUNG NEGRO I HAVE MET, A LOVE SONG:

How can I explain?
But you
Remind me of our blues . . .
My blues—*your* blues—
Ours
Singing out in a Harlem afternoon . . .

Of your own—
You carry your head a certain way
And laugh a certain way—
"Reserved" . . .

You
Are the kind who stands up to speak in church
About the housing conditions
The price of living or
In protest of the latest lynching
And wise old ladies in the front rows
All starched and holy in their white uniforms

Look so proud at you and their eyes shine:
"Our youth," they say
Our bea*ut*iful youth!"
And that is *you*

You who neither look nor sound the blues
You who bear no scars of slavery
Have never shouted out in redemption and—never will
You

You remind me of Africa
There is little that is Africa about you
Neither color nor speech nor ways of dress . . .
Yet as our people remind me of Africa
So do you . . .

I would dream of draping you in our robes
Put an ancient chant upon your lips.
It is that so much—without being so—
You are so very much *us*

And that is why I love you.

LIGHT UP *on* THIRD BLACK WOMAN,
a mother in her thirties.

MOTHER

. . . I can be coming from eight hours on an assembly line or
fourteen hours in Mrs. Halsey's kitchen. I can be all filled up
that day with three hundred years of rage so that my eyes
are flashing and my flesh is trembling—and the white boys
in the streets, they look at me and think of sex. They look
at me and that's *all* they think . . . Baby, you could be
Jesus in drag—but if you're brown they're sure you're
selling!

11.

. . . And so, dear Edythe, in the main I'd say Frank Lloyd
Wright knew his apples—or at least his prunes. And I think
that is why I did write you tonight beginning without knowing, groping a little . . . I wonder about you—I didn't just
pick out a name. I *want* to hear from you (tell me something
to read once again).

And yet . . . so very much has happened since Wisconsin
—from both ends of our two lives I am sure—that we might be
at a loss in any kind of conversation. You, I imagine, are still
quite rich with the hopes for a thriving theater in the U.S.,
and I in my own way dream of such a theater also, but somehow in a discussion I think I know what would happen. I
would recall the picketlines and demonstrations I have seen
and been in; I would recall the horsemen I have seen riding
down human beings in Times Square because they were pro-
testing lynching . . . (My preaching days are over so don't
expect any.)

I do reflect quite often on the wild miscalculations of the
Langdon Manor discussions. How farfetched we all were, the
sophisticated and the naive alike. But in this time permit only
this: We used to, all of us, chide the hearty leftists amongst us
for so carelessly referring to their beloved phrase for the
enemy: "*Fascist.*" But, dear friend, both of us in whatever our

present day thinking must admit, in our America today we can, in truth, smell it in the air . . . and how foul it is.

Certainly I feel closer to what is happening than you perhaps yet feel. I know many who have already been lapped up by this new Reich terror . . . know the arrests in the early morning, the shifty-eyed ones who follow, follow, follow . . . and know the people who are the victims: the quiet and the courageous. Frankly, I would not have thought the caliber of humanity to be so sturdy after such spheres of corruption have surrounded it. But it is so.

Quite simply and quietly as I know how to say it: I am sick of poverty, lynching, stupid wars and the universal maltreatment of my people and obsessed with a rather desperate desire for a new world for me and my brothers. Supposed to get married about September. Spirit: Happy and defiant.

Love,

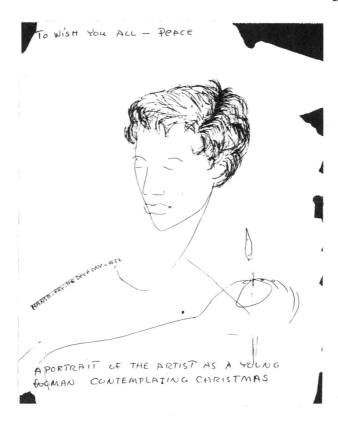

VIII

I Am a Writer,
I Am Going to Write.

5936 South Parkway
Chicago 37, Ill.
December 26, 1952

My Dear Bob,

Once again I wrote you a very long letter—the important
simple things which it said were that I have finally admitted
to myself that I *do* love you; it said I have a terrific, no, exciting idea for a play; it said that this homecoming was a blip
. . . and I went into great detail about the midnight Church
services, our Xmas tree and dirty, dismal Dreiseresque Chicago. Anyhow I decided it was a lot of crap I can tell you
myself (except about loving you and missing you—I shan't
ever have the courage to say that face to face except under
certain conditions which I will also discuss with you)—so I
destroyed it (the letter)—and this breezy little missile comes in
its stead.

I am returning to New York, the most important thing
about this trip being the long train ride here which cleared my
head so that for the first time I thought certain things through
to some basic conclusions. They go thusly:
First about "my work":
1. I am a writer. I am going to write . . .

2.

Sunday Night so very
late . . . Summer 1954

My Own Dear Husband—

I am sitting here in this miserable little bungalow, in this
miserable camp that I once loved so much, feeling cold, useless,
frustrated, helpless, disillusioned, angry and tired . . .
Bobby, I have been in love with beauty all my life—and I
guess it is always around. And already in these two weeks
I have found some things I keep close to my fondness for this
place. The land remains overwhelming—the hills, the trees,

sunrise and sunset—the lake, the moon and the stars—summer clouds . . . The poets have been right in all these centuries, darling; even in its astounding imperfection this earth of ours is magnificent. But oh this human race!

I can hear the sounds you must be uttering in response to this last remark—but this is the way I feel right now. I tell you there is much to hurt and astound the innocent heart in this world . . . much, much, much. A couple of days I didn't want to do anything but build a tree house and forget it. You know what I mean—there are times when you are sure that the peace in symphonies, and grass and light and mountains, is not to be found in this life—and honey that is a desperate feeling. . . .

3.

Sometimes in this country maybe just walking down a Southside street . . .

Or maybe suddenly up in a Harlem window . . .

Or maybe in a flash turning the page of one of those picture books from the South you will see it—

Beauty . . . stark and full . . .

No *part* of something this—but rather, Africa, simply Africa. These thighs and arms and flying wingèd cheekbones, these hallowed eyes—without negation or apology. . . .

A classical people demand a classical art.

4.

Monday, March 10

Roberto Mio—

I am enclosing the note I did not send to you to give you an indication of my immediate reaction to your being gone . . .
    (Mon Chere—
      —Whatever are you doing there? I am frightened and lonely in this house without you here.
    Write to me immediately.
                          L.)

I can tell you now that that was a positively horrible Saturday that you all left on that damn thing . . . I am now convinced that they should be banned. I watched you load and taxi away and went and got in the car and kissed poor little Spicey, my orphaned dog I thought—it seemed to me every plane near that airport almost smashed into something before I got away from the area.

YOU ARE NEVER TO FLY AGAIN.

And you certainly took your time about wiring. I had started listening to the radio for you know what—really!

Oh well.

The house, so far, reflects my varying moods to a t. Sometimes it has been unbelievably orderly—and other times as though Custer fought here . . . I have the Picasso lady up over the couch. A little incongruous on these scarred walls, but a lovely framing job nonetheless.

All told I have been fairly bored and lonely. Wish to God I could drink. (I have re-read my play a couple of times to my disgust. Had a new idea—a libretto. But have quietly resolved —yes, I will piddle around with a libretto after (1) the play is finished—(2) my novel is WELL underway—I mean it!)

Do have a good time. Of course I miss you.

Love,

P.S.—The truth is much of it *is* labored—much, however, reads well—and for the first time begins to approximate what I thought I wanted to say. Above all—I am beginning to think of the people *as people* . . . I talk to them now and all that sort of thing. I am either cracking or turning into a fugging genius. You decide.

5.

Chicago—Christmas 1955
. . . the late hours

. . . My work. It is only here on paper that I dare say it like that: "My work!"—So many truths seem to be rushing at me as the result of things felt and seen and lived through. Oh what I think I must tell this world! Oh the time that I crave— and the peace—and the *power!*

6.

April 1957

INTERIM

When I will have conquered all my days
When I shall have become mistress of the miseries of ordinary

When I will have pummelled trouble into nothing
And fashioned the atoms of unqualified despair into a star
  of hope

When I will have made the agony of hours a lovely thing
And all the aching griefs of solitude a sweet and simple song
  Why then

Death come and move with me to some other land
For I shall be ready then.

7.

Christmas again . . .

Thomas Wolfe. I don't know what I would have to go on if he
had not gone before. It has become a sweet promise, hiding, whispering to me daily . . . fame! I shock myself with such thoughts
and shake my head with embarrassment . . . fame!
Such are my days . . . longings, longings, longings . . . I want
the world to love my singing. Whether I am less for it or no—
I want it!

8.

Hotel Taft
New Haven, Conn.
January 19, 1959

Dear Mother,

Well—here we are. I am sitting alone in a nice hotel room in
New Haven, Conn. Downstairs, next door in the Shubert
Theatre, technicians are putting the finishing touches on a

living room that is supposed to be a Chicago living room. Wednesday the curtain goes up at 8 P.M. The next day the New Haven papers will say what they think about our efforts. A great deal of money has been spent and a lot of people have done some hard, hard work, and it may be the beginning of many different careers.

The actors are very good and the director is a very talented man—so if it is a poor show I won't be able to blame a soul but your youngest daughter.

Mama, it is a play that tells the truth about people, Negroes and life and I think it will help a lot of people to understand how we are just as complicated as they are—and just as mixed up—but above all, that we have among our miserable and downtrodden ranks—people who are the very essence of human dignity. That is what, after all the laughter and tears, the play is supposed to say. I hope it will make you very proud. See you soon. Love to all.

IX

Curtain Going Up at Eight

1.

LIGHT UP on BENEATHA YOUNGER,
*seated in dejection on a packing
crate, and* RUTH, *who stands nervously watching* MAMA. *Lost in
thought, the older woman holds a
little potted plant that has been
tied with sticks and cord for a
journey that may never be. Presently* WALTER *enters, slumps in
the doorway, his coat hanging
from him.*

MAMA
Where you been, son?

WALTER
(*Breathing hard*)
Made a call.

MAMA
To who, son?

WALTER
To The Man.

MAMA
What man, baby?

WALTER
The Man, Mama. Don't you know who The Man is?

RUTH
(*Cutting in quickly*)
Walter Lee . . . ?

WALTER
The Man. Like the guys in the streets say—The Man. Captain
Boss. Mistuh Charlie . . . Old Captain Please Mr. Boss-
man . . .

95

BENEATHA
(*Suddenly*)

Lindner!

WALTER
That's right! That's good. I told him to come right over.

BENEATHA
(*Fiercely, understanding*)
For what? What do you want to see him for!

WALTER
We going to do business with that man.

MAMA
What you talking 'bout, son?

WALTER
Talking 'bout life, Mama. You all always asking me to see life
like it is. Well—I laid in there on my back today . . . and
I figured it out. Life just like it is. He who gets and he who
don't get.

(*He sits down with his coat on and laughs*)
Mama, you know it's all divided up. Life is. Between the
takers and the "tooken."

(*He looks around at them*)
Yeah. And some of us are always getting "took."

(*He laughs*)
And you know why? 'Cause we all mixed up. Mixed up bad.
We get to looking 'round for the right and the wrong; and
we worry about it and cry about it and stay up nights trying
to figure out 'bout the wrong and the right of things all the
time . . . And all the time, man, them takers is out there
operating, just taking and taking . . .

RUTH
(*Coming toward him slowly*)
Walter Lee, you talking 'bout taking them people's money to
keep us from moving in our new house?

96

WALTER

I ain't just talking 'bout it, baby—I'm telling you that's what's going to happen. There ain't nothing but taking in this world, and he who takes most is smartest—

RUTH

Walter, no—

WALTER

—and it don't make a damn bit of difference *how*.

RUTH

(*In terror*)

No Walter! We gotta move. Lena, tell him. . . .

(*Turning from one to the other the words pouring out with urgency and desperation*)

Tell him, Lena—tell him we can still move. We got four grown people in this house—we can work. Walter—I'll work . . . I'll work twenty hours a day in all the kitchens in Chicago . . . I'll strap my baby on my back if I have to and scrub all the floors in America and wash all the sheets in America if I have to—but we got to move . . . We got to get out of here. . . .

WALTER

You don't understand, baby—you still don't understand—them people out there where you want us to move is so upset they willing to pay us *not* to move—and we gonna help 'em. That white man is going to walk in that door able to write checks for more money that we ever had—

MAMA

(*Rising and coming toward him*)

Son—how come you talk so much 'bout money?

WALTER

(*With immense passion*)

Because it is life, Mama!

MAMA
(*Very quietly*)
Oh—so now it's life. Money is life. Once upon a time freedom
used to be life—now it's money. I guess the world really do
change . . .

WALTER
No—it was always money, Mama. We just didn't know it.

MAMA
Son—I come from five generations of people who was slaves
and sharecroppers—but ain't nobody in my family never let
nobody pay 'em no money that was a way of telling us we
wasn't fit to walk the earth. We ain't never been that poor.
(*Turning away from him*)
We ain't never been that dead inside.

WALTER
What's the matter with you all! I didn't make this world! It
was give to me exactly this way! Hell, yes, I want me some
yachts someday! Yes, I want to hang some real pearls 'round
my wife's neck. Ain't she supposed to wear no pearls? Somebody tell me—tell me, who decides which woman is suppose
to wear pearls in this world. I tell you I am a *man*—and I
think my wife should wear some pearls in this world!

MAMA
Baby, how you going to feel on the inside?

WALTER
Fine! . . . Going to feel fine . . . like a man . . .

MAMA
You won't have nothing left then, Walter Lee.

WALTER
(*Coming to her*)
I'm going to feel fine, Mama. I'm going to look that son-of-a-
bitch in the eyes and say—
(*He falters*)
—and say, "All right, Mr. Lindner—

(He falters even more)
—that's your neighborhood out there. You got the right to keep it like you want. You got the right to have it like you want. Just write the check and—the house is yours." And—and I am going to say—
(His voice almost breaks)
"And you—you people just put the money in my hand and you won't have to live next to this bunch of stinking niggers! . . ."
(He straightens up and moves away from his mother, walking around the room)
Maybe—maybe I'll just get down on my black knees . . .
(He does so; RUTH, BENNIE and MAMA watch him in frozen horror)
"Captain, Mistuh, Bossman—
(He starts groveling, grinning, and wringing his hands in profoundly anguished imitation of the stereotype)
"A-hee-hee-hee! Yasssssuh! Great White Father, just gi' ussen de money, fo' God's Sake, and we's ain't gwine come out deh and dirty up yo' white folks neighborhood!" And I'll feel fine . . . fine . . . fine!

> LIGHT DIMS *on the* YOUNGERS, *frozen in position, with* WALTER *still on his knees.*

2.

> *Onto the stage, framed by the* YOUNGERS, *strides the young black woman, speech in hand, who concluded the Prologue.*

PLAYWRIGHT

Good evening. I am very pleased to have been invited to be a part of this Negro Writers' Conference . . . I suppose I have been invited because my first play will be opening soon . . . I think *I* like it but I've no idea what the public will think of it. Still, for the moment, let's presume I am a writer.

(Now—as before—she refers to the typed speech she has been carrying)

I must share with you a part of a conversation I had with a young New York intellectual in my living room in Greenwich Village. "Why," he said to me, "are you so sure the human race should go on? You do not believe in a prior arrangement of life on this planet. You know perfectly well that the *reason* for survival does not exist in nature!" . . .

I answered him the only way I could: that man is unique in the universe, the only creature who has in fact the power to transform the universe. Therefore, it did not seem unthinkable to me that man might just do what the apes never will—*impose* the reason for life on life. That is what I said to my friend. I wish to live because life has within it that which is good, that which is beautiful and that which is love. Therefore, since I have known all of these things, I have found them to be reason enough and—I wish to live. Moreover, because this is so, I wish others to live for generations and generations and generations . . .

3.

LIGHT UP *on the* YOUNGERS, *as before.* WALTER *slowly rises. The* PLAYWRIGHT *stands watching as, through the door, bursts Walter's young son* TRAVIS.

TRAVIS
(With great excitement)
Grandmama—the moving men are downstairs! The truck just pulled up.

MAMA
(Turning and looking at him)
Are they, baby? They downstairs?
(SHE sighs and sits. TRAVIS *looks from one to another in bewilderment. Presently a middle-aged white man appears in the open doorway. It is* KARL LINDNER, *hat and briefcase in hand. He knocks lightly, to gain attention, and comes in.)*

LINDNER

Uh—hello . . .

RUTH
(*to* WALTER)

He's here.

(*He looks up but does not move*)

LINDNER
(*Coming to the table with efficiency, opening his briefcase and starting to unfold papers and unscrew fountain pen*)
Well, I was certainly glad to hear from you people.
(*A long moment passes.* WALTER *does not move*)
Life can really be so much simpler than people let it be most of the time . . . Well—with whom do I negotiate? You, Mrs. Younger, or your son here?
(MAMA *sits with her hands folded on her lap and her eyes closed as* WALTER *passes the back of his sleeve across his mouth, and, at last, advances slowly and awkwardly.* TRAVIS *goes up to* LINDNER *curiously*)
Just some official papers, sonny.

RUTH
Travis, you go downstairs.

MAMA
(*Opening her eyes and looking into* WALTER'S)
No, Travis, you stay right here. And you make him understand what you doing, Walter Lee. You teach him good. You show him where our five generations done come to.
(WALTER *hesitates—looking from her to the boy*)
Go ahead, son. Go ahead—
(TRAVIS *grins at his father, who at last draws him beside him and faces* LINDNER)

WALTER
Well, Mr. Lindner . . .

101

(BENEATHA turns away)
We called you—
(He looks down into his son's eyes and a profound, simple groping quality comes into his speech)
—because, well, me and my family—
(He looks around again and shifts from one foot to the other)
Well—we are very plain people . . .

LINDNER
Yes—

WALTER
I mean—I have worked as a chauffeur most of my life—and my wife here, she does domestic work in people's kitchens. So does my mother. I mean—we are plain people . . .

LINDNER
(Absorbed in documents)
Yes, Mr. Younger—

WALTER
(Looking down at his shoes and then up at the man)
And—uh—well, my father, well, he was a laborer most of his life.

LINDNER
(Absolutely confused)
Uh, yes—

WALTER
My father almost beat a man to death once because this man called him a bad name or something, you know what I mean?

LINDNER
No, I'm afraid I don't.

WALTER
(Coming fully erect)
Well, what I mean is that we come from people who had a lot of pride. I mean—we are very proud people. And that's my

sister over there and she's going to be a doctor—and we are very proud—

LINDNER

Well—I am sure that is very nice, but—

WALTER

(*Facing the man eye to eye*)

What I am telling you is that we called you over here to tell you . . . And this—this is my son—

(*Father and son exchange brief glances*)

And he makes the sixth generation of our family in this country—and we have all thought about your offer and we have decided to move into our house because my father—my father—he earned it for us brick by brick.

(MAMA *has her eyes closed and is rocking back and forth as though she were in church, with her head nodding the Amen yes*)

We don't want to make no trouble for nobody or fight no causes and we will try to be good neighbors.

(*He looks the man absolutely in the eyes*)

We don't want your money.

(*He turns and walks away*)

LINDNER

(*Looking around at all of them*)

I take it then—I take it that you have decided to occupy—

BENEATHA

That's what the *man* said.

LINDNER

(*Appealing to* MAMA)

Mrs. Younger, you are older and wiser—

MAMA

(*Openly beaming*)

You know how these young folks is nowadays, mister. Can't do a thing with 'em!

(*Abruptly, as he opens his mouth—*)

Goodbye.

LIGHTS OUT *on all but the* PLAY-WRIGHT

4.

GIN BI

PLAYWRIGHT

Months before I had turned the last page out of the typewriter and pressed all the sheets neatly together in a pile, and gone and stretched out face down on the living room floor. I had finished a play; a play I had no reason to think or not think would ever be done; a play that I was sure no one would quite understand. . . .

I cannot any longer remember if I liked it or not. I have said to some that it was not my "kind" of play; and yet it moved me to read it sometimes—and once I wept at a performance.

I have been tongue-tied and glib and fatuous trying to answer questions which must always seem strange to a writer: "Why did you write it?" and "How did it come to be?"

The truly relevant and revealing answers are always too diffuse, too vague in time and place and specific meaning to quite try and share with people. *I* know—but how can I tell it?

104

JUNO

Oh Blessed Virgin, where were you when me darlin' son was riddled with bullets! . . . Sacred Heart of the Crucified Jesus, take away our hearts o' stone . . . an' give us hearts of flesh!

PLAYWRIGHT

I was seventeen and I did not think then of writing the melody as *I* knew it—in a different key; but I believe it entered my consciousness and stayed there.

LIGHT UP *on* MAMA—*as before*

MAMA

When you starts measuring somebody, measure him right, child, measure him right. Make sure you done taken into account what hills and valleys he come through before he got to wherever he is. . . .

PLAYWRIGHT

. . . How can one adequately tell *that?*

CURTAIN

PART TWO

"... For Generations and Generations and Generations"

I ❖

...A Slight Sense of Justification for Being...

VOGUE MAGAZINE, THE CONDÉ NAST PUBLICATIONS INC.

PHOTO BY DAVID ATTIE

PEOPLE ARE TALKING ABOUT . . .

LORRAINE HANSBERRY, author of that direct hit, *A Raisin in the Sun,* winner of the New York Drama Critics Circle award for the best American play of the season. Although caught in the pounce of publicity, she has remained a quiet woman who lives three flights up in a Greenwich Village walk-up with her husband, a song-writer and music publisher. Her creation now brings her ten percent of the weekly gross of $41,000, a big whack of the $300,000 that Columbia Pictures has paid for the movie rights, plus handsome financial arrangements as writer of the movie script. She will write most of that script in her Bleecker Street apartment. There, the small rooms are jammed with living. Records rest on the floor, nuts in a bowl, pennies in a dish, and, on the walls, reproductions of a Picasso, a Gauguin, a Michelangelo. In the photograph opposite, the sculptured figure was done by Miss Hansberry when she was a sophomore at the University of Wisconsin. Her writing clothes are still rather campus—white, beat sneakers, thick white socks, chino pants. At the New York opening of her play, however, she wore beautiful black with a rope of pearls, heard her sophisticated mother, in from Chicago, say "That's my daughter," as the applause continued until the great Sidney Poitier pulled the girl from the audience to take her bows. . . .

—*Vogue Magazine,* June, 1959

1.

PROJECTION of LORRAINE HANSBERRY and her recorded voice in the midst of an interview.

. . . I'm very, very lucky, of course, to be only approaching thirty-one at the moment, and to have had the opportunity, you know, to see it put before many people and have their reactions to it. And there is nothing yet that has been written, I don't think, in poetry or song, that has quite articulated the gratification of that. It probably is the most fulfilling experience a human being can have—to try and create something and to have it received with any measure of recognition for the effort. So that I can only say it in personal terms: I get an enormous sense of personal fulfillment and—a slight sense of justification for being. . . .

111

2.

Dear Friends, thank you!

Thank you on behalf of our entire company; your beautiful tribute and lovely award are part of the statement we hoped we were offering to the American theater.

I cannot adequately tell you what recognition and tribute mean to the young writer and, I am sure, to the young artist of all fields. One works, one dreams, and, if one is lucky, one actually produces. But true fulfillment only comes when our fellows say: "Ah, we understand, we appreciate, we enjoy.". . .

3.

INTERVIEWER
And what about success—this little goddess Success?

L. H.

I think it's wonderful, it's wonderful and I'm enjoying it. I think there comes a time, you know, when you pull the telephone out and you go off and you end it. But for the time being I'm enjoying every bit of it. I've tried to go to everything I've been invited to and—I shouldn't even say this on the air—but so far I've tried to answer every piece of correspondence I get, which, as I said in the *New Yorker* piece, gets to be about twenty or thirty pieces a day at this point. . . .

4.

Dear Miss Hansberry:

After having read and enjoyed *A Raisin in the Sun* several times, I have decided to ask for your help in an assignment. I am a senior at Kubasaki High School on Okinawa and am taking Drama One. . . .

Dear Miss Hansberry,

. . . I'm a white native Georgian and I thought it was a wonderful play—and most informative from the Negro's viewpoint. I understand the moral, but I can't imagine what the

112

future holds for this family. I wonder if you can explain whether the white neighborhood supposedly accepts them, or whether life continues to be the futile struggle it has always been for them. . . .

Dear Miss Hansberry—

Would you please send me your autograph . . . if you are as nice as you look I know I shall receive it.

Your faithful follower,

P. S. I have scores of Playwrights among my 4650 names. . . .

Dear Miss Hansberry,

I'm one of the nine students that attended Little Rock Central High School. . . . I guess you could call this a crude try at my first fan letter. I wish all the students could have seen the play before entering Central in '57. It would have made us prouder to enter Central because we knew we were not the only Walter Lee Youngers.

Sincerely,

5.

INTERVIEWER
The question, I'm sure, is asked you many times—you may be tired of it—someone comes up to you and says: "This is not really a Negro play; why, this could be about anybody! It's a play about people!" What is your reaction? What do you say?

L. H.
Well, I hadn't noticed the contradiction because I'd always been under the impression that Negroes *are* people. But actually it's an excellent question, because invariably that has been the point of reference. And I do know what people are trying to say. People are trying—what they are trying to say is that this is not what they consider the traditional treatment of the

113

Negro in the theater. They're trying to say that it isn't a propaganda play, that it isn't something that hits you over the head; they are trying to say that they believe the characters in our play transcend category. However, it is an unfortunate way to try and say it, because I believe that one of the most sound ideas in dramatic writing is that in order to create the universal, you must pay very great attention to the specific. Universality, I think, emerges from truthful identity of what is.

In other words, I have told people that not only is this a Negro family, specifically and definitely culturally, but it's not even a New York family or a southern Negro family. It is specifically Southside Chicago . . . that kind of care, that kind of attention to detail. In other words, I think people, to the extent we accept them and believe them as who they're supposed to be, to that extent they can become everybody. So I would say it is definitely a Negro play before it is anything else. . . .

6.

April 4, 1960

State Theatre
Ostrava, Czechoslovakia

Dear Mr. Chuchvalec:

I cannot describe to you the great joy it gives me to know that my play has been committed to the language of Capek; my only sadness is that my cultural illiteracy will not allow me to read it in what, I am told, is your excellent translation.

I have never had the opportunity to visit your great country and to salute your historically dynamic people. I hope that some day I shall be able to do so, but until such time it gives me enormous pleasure to be a source of communication between our two cultures via your four concurrent productions of my play. I was deeply moved to receive the album with the photos and program notes. I am excited and anticipant now for word of its reception. . . .

7.

. . . Thank you so much for your perceptive and kind remarks tonight. I am struck by the depth of your understanding of our play as expressed by your citation remarks. I think they showed genuine understanding rather than mere back-slapping—which I don't turn down either, however!

As you perceive, I am one who considers the worship of Despair a pointless and, I must add, a rather boring pursuit. As for its kinsman, Obscurity, it is clear that it enjoys a fraudulent stature from time to time in human cultural history, but it merely serves to impale and distort the true purposes and joys of art. I am audacious enough to go on supposing that Shakespeare probably rejoiced for whatever he was able to *reveal* about the human experience rather than the reverse.

On the other hand, I am the first to say that ours is a complex and difficult country and some of our complexities are indeed grotesque. We who are Negro Americans can offer that last remark with unwavering insistence. It is, on the other hand, also a great nation with certain beautiful and indestructible traditions and potentials which can be seized by all of us who possess imagination and love of man. There is, as a certain play suggests, a great deal to be fought in America—but, at the same time, there is so much which begs to be but re-affirmed and cherished with sweet defiance.

Vulgarity, blind conformity and mass lethargy need not triumph in the land of Lincoln and Frederick Douglass and Walt Whitman and Mark Twain. There is simply no reason why dreams should dry up like raisins or prunes or anything else in America. If you will permit me to say so, I believe that we can *impose* beauty on our future. . . .

8.

The Detroit Free Press
Detroit 31, Michigan
March 25, 1959

Dear Miss Hansberry,

In a lifetime of reading and play-going this is the first time I have felt compelled to write to an author. And last Saturday afternoon at the Barrymore Theatre is the first time I have wanted to rush onstage and embrace the whole cast. I'm sure the dehumidifiers must be working overtime, because seven kinds of tears were flying around the orchestra. And I—who ordinarily keep my wits about me—went back to my hotel and got in the shower with my wristwatch on. But . . . the experience was worth every penny of the repair bill.

Best of luck to you. You're on the right track, and I hope to see much more of your work.

Sincerely,
Lillian Jackson Braun
Living Section Editor

Barrymore Theatre
March 31, 1959

Dear Mrs. Braun:

I don't know—I just sort of particularly liked your note; aside from the really kind compliments I think the Wrist-Watch Question absolutely charmed me.

Do not ever let any of the would be sophisticates in this world tell you that correspondences like yours do not mean everything in the world to someone like me. Because I am here to say that they most certainly do.

Thank you—thank you,

9.

My dear Miss Oehler:

. . . Let us please be quite clear about one thing: I have treated Mr. Lindner as a human being merely because he is one; that does not make the meaning of his call less malignant, less sick. I could no more imagine myself allowing the Youngers to accept his obscene offer of money than I could imagine myself allowing them to accept a cash payment for their own murder.

You seem to wish to quarrel with me about what you consider fuzzy-headed notions of idealism. I absolutely plead guilty to the charge of idealism. But simple idealism. You see, our people don't really have a choice. We must come out of the ghettoes of America, because the ghettoes are killing us; not only our dreams, as Mama says, but our very bodies. It is not an abstraction to us that the average American Negro has a life expectancy of five to ten years less than the average white. You see, Miss Oehler, that is murder, and a Negro writer cannot be expected to share the placid view of the situation that might be the case with a white writer.

As for changing "the hearts of individuals"—I am glad the American nation did not wait for the hearts of individual slave owners to change to abolish the slave system—for I suspect that I should still be running around on a plantation as a slave. And that really would not do.

Sincerely,

117

10.

NOTE TO THE POSTMAN *

POSTMAN, PLEASE NOTE:
CENT EXTRA POSTAGE
HAS BEEN PAID FOR THIS
WEIGHT. ONLY
14¢ IS DUE FOR EDUCATIONAL
MATERIAL. THESE WERE THE
ONLY STAMPS I HAD. THERE-
FORE THE GOVT. CAME
OUT AHEAD THIS TIME.
SO—GIVE THE NEXT
POOR FELLOW A
BREAK WHEN
HE IS SHORT,
PLEASE?

11.

Dear Mr. Ashworth:

. . . I think one does not get tired of anything quite so rewarding, but after a while my mind and my fingers wore out —and I learned to appreciate the letters and file them and not try to reply. This is all because I have not figured out what is to be done with a secretary when correspondence has been taken care of—so I have never employed one and probably never will.

In any case, as you can see, there are exceptions to the above.

Might I remark on the tradition now grown up amongst us concerning what *you* call "Domestic realism." I think myself that American intellectual thought has been pretty much fractured by the Great Retreat. From everything. From everything, that is, that smacks of passionate partisanship. A host of labels have been created which are supposed to insulate our mentalities from "Clichés" and "Dogmas." The marvel is that all the suspect clichés and dogmas under attack have a way of

* Scrawled on the outside of a Manila envelope.

118

always turning out to be those which have been used (and, heaven knows, mis-used) in an effort to say that things are still pretty rotten in Denmark. That is—"thesis plays" and "social plays" are supposed to be, by this reasoning, plays which plead a cause. We have grown so accustomed to this abuse of language and ideas that most people try to explain *why* that is so and do not understand that there are *no* plays which are not social and no plays that do not have a thesis. (That is hardly a revolutionary observation so it is quite interesting that it is such an unpopular one.) The fact of the matter is that Arthur Miller and Lillian Hellman and Henrik Ibsen are no more social playwrights than Tennessee Williams and Bill Inge and Friedrich Dürrenmatt—or anybody else. Noel Coward writes social plays and so does Jerome Chodorov and Arthur Laurents; and so did, of course, William Shakespeare— and so did the fashioners of the Commedia dell'Arte in Italy way back, etc.

The problem is that there are great plays and lousy plays and reasonably good plays; when the artist achieves a force of art which is commensurate with his message—he hooks us. When he doesn't, we are bored or offended about being lectured to, and confused because we think it must be the "Message" which is out of place—or uninteresting or trivial or ridiculous because of the clumsy way he has hurled it at us. The fact is—if he really had nothing he wanted to tell us; nothing he wanted to persuade us of; no partisanship he wanted to evoke—well, he wouldn't have written a play. He would have just sat around grunting in a dark corner; sans people, sans ideas even perhaps—sans everything which I think is life on earth—that is, above the sod.

Of course, whatever is said must be said through the living arguments of human beings in conflict with other human beings, with themselves, with the abstractions which seem to them to be "their society." Of course! But that narrows nothing and enlarges everything. The more swiftly that American drama comes to believe that my dramatic experience will be larger when I know *why* the pathetic chap has turned to alcohol and not merely that he has; why to heroin; why to prostitution, despair, decadent preoccupations—the more swiftly, I insist, our drama will gain more meaningful stature. The fact of the matter is that we are all surrounded by the elements of profound tragedy in contemporary life, no less than were

Shakespeare and the Greeks, but that thus far we (the dramatists, all of us, I think) are still confounded by its elusive
properties and colossal dimensions. In certain peculiar ways
we have been conditioned to think not small—but tiny. And
the thing, I think, which has strangled us most is the tendency
to turn away from the world in the search for the universe.
That is chaos in science; can it be anything else in art?

Thank you so very much for your letter. It did not ask for
this barrage of opinion and conversation—but by its tone I am
sure you are the sort of theater-goer who also likes to talk.

Sincerely,

13.

August 24, 1960

New York City Mission Society
Harlem Branch
Camp Minisink
Port Jervis, N. Y.

Dear Taps. . . .

All of you, and Ma Kline and Thornie:

My gift came today and I am so delighted that I am sitting
down right now to write you a—shall we say, *lengthy* thank
you note.

I have just tried it on for the mirror (see full length portrait
@ right) and my family. They—my family, that is—left (no
imagination). But the mirror and I feel very, very chic. It is
my intention to keep it and wear it until it is a fatigued and
shredded white, to remind me of one of the most special weekends I have ever spent. And I kid you not.

Nor did I kid you in that rather dull, if quite sincere, speech
about fully expecting exceptional contributions from you, in-
dividually and collectively. It is, as I said, in your faces, in
your singing. You are expressive and full of the most infectious
joy of life I have yet come across in our country. And yet
I know you are realistic too. Do hang on to all of it. The entire
community of New York City should be grateful to the two

marvelous people most responsible for helping to give you such excellent starting grounds.

I wish every one of you long, long, happy, productive and creative lives. And sincerely hope I will meet up with you again.

Affectionately,

P. S. Special greetings to those of you who have written. I am keeping the letters. And a special greeting to Nurse, her medicine was as effective as it was dangerous looking.

II ❖

The Human Race
Concerns Me

1.

INTERVIEWER

Miss Hansberry, I want to close with a personal question, a quite simple and factual one: What are your plans for the future? What do you work on next?

L. H.

Three years ago, or four years ago, whatever it was, I had written four little plays. I say "little," but they were three-act plays—I started out, never having written a play in my life, with three-act plays which, I suppose, was a hangover from my painting days when I never could start anything other than, you know, the whole thing at one time and just—wham —into it. And now—well, I want to continue the process; I want to continue just tackling things and writing plays all the way out, and those that I think have some merit I will dare to read to other people, as I finally dared to read "the One". . . .

2.

PROPOSED WORK—September, 1960:

The Sign in Jenny Reed's Window, musical drama
A Revolt of Lemmings, novel
The Life of Mary Wollstonecraft, full length drama
  (*Thesis:* Strong-minded woman of rationality; & a creature of history; nonetheless, a human being, destroyed many times over by "life as she is lived")
The Marrow of Tradition, a full length drama
Les Blancs (*The Holy Ones*)
The Drinking Gourd, TV play—into stage play (?)
some short stories
The Musical
Toussaint, an opera. . . .

3.

I was obsessed with the idea of writing a play (or at that time even a novel) about the Haitian liberator Toussaint L'Ouverture when I was still an adolescent and had first come across his adventure with freedom. I thought then, with that magical sense of perception that sometimes lights up our younger years, that this was surely one of the most extraordinary personalities to pass through history. I think so now.

Since then I have discovered that it has been a widespread obsession. Neither the Haitian Revolution nor the figures of L'Ouverture or Christophe or Dessalines have gone wanting in dramatic or other fictional materials. Those I have troubled to read, however, have offended my early dream. The exotic, the voodoo mysticism, the over-rich sensuality which springs to mind traditionally with regard to Caribbean peoples has outlandishly been allowed to outweigh and, to my mind, distort the entire significance and genuine romance of the Haitian Revolution and its heroes.

The people of Haiti waged a war and won it. They created a nation out of a savagely dazzling colonial jewel in the mighty French empire. The fact of their achievement, of the wresting of national freedom from one of the most powerful nations on the face of the earth by lowly, illiterate and cruelly divided black slaves has its own core of monumental drama. One need not bow to the impulse to embellish it with romantic racism.

Thus, I began work two years ago. I shall consider *Toussaint* my "epic" effort because in this I intend to depart from the traditional canonization of historical heroes, and try, with all my heart, to write a man—and yet, at the same time, not lose the wonder of his magnitude, his telling affirmation. L'Ouverture was not a god; he was a man. And by the will of one man in union with a multitude Santo Domingo was transformed; aye—the French empire, the western hemisphere, the history of the United States: therefore, the world.

Such then is the will and the power of man—and perhaps the secret of the greatness of humankind. . . .

4.

> MUSIC—*the fragile tinkle of an eighteenth-century French minuet being played somewhere offstage on a harpsichord.*
> LIGHTS SLOWLY UP. *The upstairs bedroom of the Great House of a*

sugar plantation on Santo Domingo, 1780—the year of insurrection; the year before major rebellion. Beyond and below is the Bay of Cap Français: a serene blue water edged by the curving dark "land of mountains" first called "Haiti"—as it will be again. BAYON DE BERGIER *stands, in a state of unfinished dress, at the balcony, with his hands resting on the grill of exquisite Spanish ironwork. His wife,* LUCIE, *reclines on a chaise, so swathed in filmy boudoir fabric that it is difficult, at first, to discern her person from the cushions that surround her. But as she talks, now and again, a hand rises and floats through the air.* BAYON *turns and regards her with exaggerated impatience, then demonstratively crosses downstage to resume his dressing.*

BAYON

I will ring for Destine now so that you may get up and begin your toilette.

(SHE *stretches lazily but says nothing.* HE *sighs, hunting about in bureau drawers for items of his costume.*)

Where are my garters?

(SHE *smiles, says nothing*)

Where are my garters?

LUCIE

Why are you so sullen—I've changed my mood, why don't you change yours?

BAYON

I am not being sullen; I am looking for my garters.

127

LUCIE

If you were a true gentleman you would have someone dress
you.

(HE *sighs heavily*)

How you do sigh of late, Bayon. You have turned into one
long sigh.

> (*There is the sudden crack of a whip off-
> stage and the piercing cry of a human being
> in pain. The minuet halts for the merest
> fraction of a moment and then resumes as a
> second, and a third cry are heard.* BAYON
> *finds his garters.*)

Who is your Toussaint having punished now?

BAYON

Simion is being whipped.

LUCIE

Toussaint is a brute.

BAYON

He is a steward and an excellent one.

LUCIE

Do you think he gets pleasure from it?

BAYON

Oh, of course he does.

LUCIE

Personally—I don't think so. I have watched his merciless ways
with the slaves—and I saw no pleasure in it.

BAYON

What then?

LUCIE

A woman's reasoning, as you always say. It would bore you
or make you laugh to hear about it. I will keep it to myself.

BAYON

Excellent. I for one know only that I have a steward who knows how to drive men.

LUCIE

What?

BAYON

I said that I have a steward who knows how to drive slaves.

LUCIE

But that isn't what you said the first time. You said—"men." But isn't there a difference between slaves and other men, Bayon?

BAYON

In the sense that I was speaking it is all the same.

LUCIE

(*Reflectively, hardly having listened to what he has just replied*)

I saw him once when he was having Sidilie whipped. He stood quite near, with his arms folded across his chest, watching with the most complicated expression on his face that I have ever seen. . . .

BAYON

Oh, yes, yes—he is a weird old buck, if that's what you mean. Toussaint has his own sense of the order of things.

LUCIE

Yes, I think so.

(*Tilting her head the least little bit*)

What would become of the plantation if he ever ran away, Bayon?

BAYON

He never will. He is content. He does his work and I give him plenty of leisure for his walks in the woods and his little mumble jumble business. That is all that is required.

LUCIE

Could it be possible, Bayon, that if Toussaint knows how to command men, not merely slaves, since you use the words as the same, that he may command even you?

BAYON

No—that is not even remotely possible. I command. He is my steward. Toussaint is a special kind of black.
(*Looking off*)
There is some passive—almost mystical acceptance. I once asked him, you know, about the insurrection. He waved it away and seemed very impatient to hear it discussed.
(*Turning to leave*)
Now, will you dress, my sweet. I shall expect you downstairs in—

LUCIE
(*Not listening*)
How strange the two of you are together in the fields. You, in your wide-brimmed hat astride your horse, seeming to command—

BAYON
(*Turning in the door and enunciating*)
I shall expect you downstairs in at least an hour. And— in excellent humor.

LUCIE

—and he, the slave, beside you, barefoot, in that yellow handkerchief and quite hideous face: commanding!

BAYON

Now that should do, Lucie. And I have explained to you a hundred times—Toussaint is not a slave.

LUCIE

Well—is he free?

BAYON
(*Furious*)
No, he is not free either.

LUCIE

Then he must be a slave. If you are not one, you must be the other.

BAYON

It is a special situation. You are a woman. You cannot understand it.

LUCIE

Oh, but explain it to me, Bayon. I will try very hard to understand. And explain about yourself. Are *you* a free man, Bayon?

BAYON

Of course I am a free man.

LUCIE

Then why haven't you left Santo Domingo long ago? Since that is what you want more than anything else in the world —to be out of here! What is it that keeps a free man where he does not wish to be? Tell me—what is freedom, Bayon de Bergier?

BAYON

That is an abstraction that no one can answer.
(*The cries rise again and the minuet continues.*)
Least of all, these days, a Frenchman. . . .

5.

July 3, 1961—

. . . It is very hot and I am not feeling too well. Ernest Hemingway shot himself to death yesterday. How utterly mad it all is, this life business. It is so awful to live without envy of anything.

The days pass and pass and I do nothing. Such times have been before. I just sit all day or traverse the streets in pointless rounds—and then sit at this desk and smoke cigarettes. Would like to be working but am in awful trouble with it . . .

6.

September 5—

Blobby-globby days again . . . that awful jackass feeling that I suppose is inextricable from being a writer . . . The work does not go well. Would like to be with a company of friends laughing and clowning and drinking—two brave scotches and talk my fool head off. But I am alone. Very. Tonight. Seven o'clock. Spice, scotch and me. . . .

7.

She was a splendid young creature.

Oh, sure—she knew she was silly. You could tell that from her eyes: "I'm a fool!" they shouted happily. I guess that was her charm—her silliness. It was as if she knew she was beautiful. It was as if she knew she was almost perfect.

She *was* spoiled. They had spoiled her when she was very young. They were sorry sometimes—but not often. And that too was because of her eyes which, when they were not shouting "I'm a fool!", were whispering: "I am just a helpless, lovable little thing, and I love you, I am devoted to you . . . you will make me cry if you do not melt right there on the spot and caress me and act as if you love me more than anything in the world."

And they would caress her, stop whatever they were doing and caress her. And talk to her.

When one looked at her—at her splendid young body, straight, perfectly molded, eager and sure in its movements; when one watched her frolicking about of an afternoon—one could only think of youth. Watching her you dreaded even thinking of her ever getting old, ever moving slowly with caution and wisdom. It would be like the sun growing dark.

But what matter! Now she is young. And beautiful. And almost perfect . . . my "almost" collie.

And her name is Spice. . . .

132

January 13

Dear Miss Watson:

I should forewarn you that some of those closest to me (and some not so close, I am sure) feel that I am a pretty opinionated character; of the sort, you know, who smacks her lips over any situation where someone has actually *asked* my opinion. And—it's true. And, smiles aside, I hope that you will take whatever I put down here exactly that way—as one opinionated person's opinion. It is this:

I cannot imagine that you ought change the racial (or any other kind) identity of a character whom you have organically conceived as a part of a play for the "reasons" that have been suggested to you. Almost anything and everything that one might say about producers is probably true—as they are, like everybody else, of all kinds. But I personally cannot help but feel that they should make their main contribution to the theater by producing and letting the writers do the writing. I do not mean that either creativity or intelligence somehow eludes individuals who happen to be producers; of course not, but I do mean that if they wish to write plays they ought to do that on their own and not indulge in the horrendous armchair "art" of re-writing others.

I simply have no respect at all for that kind of imbalance. Then too, all the various "authorities" said (*before* all the money that my play made for an awful lot of people) that such materials were not commercially sound, nobody was going to pay those prices to see "a bunch of Negroes emoting," etc., etc. And then, of course, *after* success, another bunch of experts rose to the occasion to insist that here was the perfect example of a play *designed* to the commercial formula! So you see you can't win. And the only answer to it is your own: to completely ignore all of it and write the best that one can about whatever matter agitates one and try to strike art—and be the most grateful of creatures roaming this earth if one strikes that.

Plays are better written because one *must*, even if people think that you are being either artsy-craftsy or a plain liar if you say so. One result of this is that I usually don't say it any more, I just write—at my own dismally slow (and yes, heart-breaking and maddening) commercially disinterested pace and choice of subject matter. Which is one reason why you haven't ever heard of anything else by me. . . .

DAVID AT

9.

The Saturday evening before Easter, 1962—

Yesterday I was alone. And so, I did some work; I don't really remember what. And then in a fit of self-sufficiency went shopping in the supermarket and bought food: liver, steak, chops. I rather knew the kind of weekend that was coming. But was not depressed. . . . The being alone is better. That is what one has to learn ultimately. It really is better to be alone; it is horrible—but it is better.

Tonight worked. Productively. But can't get excited about any accomplishment tonight.

Worst of all, I am ashamed of being alone. Or is it my loneliness that I am ashamed of? I have closed the shutters so that no one can see. Me. Alone. Sitting at the typewriter on Easter Eve; brooding; alone. Upstairs I will keep the drapes drawn. No one must know these hurts. Why? I shall wash my hair. It is helping my skin. I shall be beautiful this time next year: long hair and clear skin. And I shall still be lonely. On Easter eve. At the typewriter. . . .

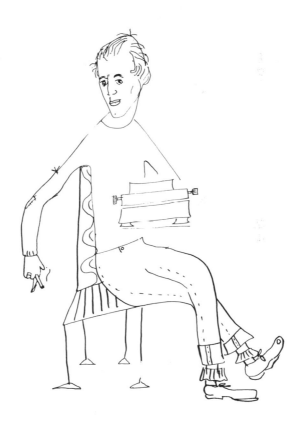

10.

Dear Leonard Melfi,

Thank you so very much for letting me read your script. It was not, I assure you, an idle effort; if I may say so, merit your play does have. I am naturally attracted to what I understood to be a qualitative humanist statement in it and you do seem to have feeling for the various kinds of hurts in most of us. I think you have it within you to write substantial drama; and I *enjoyed* reading your play.

Nobody asked me—but I would like to remark one or two negatives also (which of course are freely tossed away by any self-respecting author as I perfectly well know—but anyhow): I longed for tightness in the writing. Not for the commercial reasons—"We don't want the commuters to start rattling their programs—" and all that. But because I think we new writers are less inclined to hide our uncertainties of structure in meandering dialogue if we decide in the third re-write that every single line MUST count. Even at the expense of what we usually hope is our "mood-setting" passage. Genuine drama has a way of hiding out in the essences of scenes rather than in their trappings, I think. Also, whenever we deal with characters. . . .

11.

> LIGHT UP *on* TOUSSAINT, *in uniform—a short, wiry, very black man.*

TOUSSAINT
(*To* CHRISTOPHE)

You see, Henri, I am a very wise man and we wise men—ha! we don't make the same mistakes that ordinary men make. Take this—this Napoleon Bonaparte, for instance, this Napoleon Bonaparte and myself; we recognize one another. He is different from the others. He is the first of the Europeans to know who I am; and who the blacks of Santo Domingo are. He is that wise; he is therefore the first enemy of scale I will have matched wits with. This Bonaparte, Henri, he deserves his reputation . . .

136

12.

May 1—

Eventually it comes to you: the thing that makes you exceptional, if you are at all, is inevitably that which must also make you lonely. . . .

13.

May 22—

. . . I think that all parts of my temperament considered, I should probably find some satisfaction in renting one of those rose-surrounded cottages in the English countryside—not too far from or close to you-know-who's birthplace and all (there just might be something in that air!) But what would "this sceptred isle" make of the signpost "*Welcome to Chitterling Heights*"?

14.

May 22, 1962

Dear Ann of the Routes:

Stockholm—London—and now there you are perched on the Mediterranean! Such postmarks make me feel various things: a little sad that my traveling instincts are so cowed by mechanical things like boats and planes and a joint suspicion that it is probably just as well that I do not take my various depressions hither and thither. (Now that, as a matter of fact, is a false lead because, for some exceedingly mysterious reason, haven't been having so many depressions as all that of late.)

The truth is that I am in fairly robust spirits most of the time lately (hasn't done a *thing* for my typing though) and I have got some work done. Switch back and forth from *Toussaint* to *Jennie Reed* (who, as a matter of fact, has metamorphosized into "Iris Brustein" as the "musical drama" became a play). And have also got to meet some of the Freedom Ride leaders out of the South: my dear, what truly extraor-

137

dinary young people. They make one almost blind with re-suspicions that the human race really is—what?—*possible*, I guess. They are thrilling. . . .

15.

LIGHT UP *on the young* TOUSSAINT

TOUSSAINT
We have something in our favor, Biassou. The Europeans will always *under*estimate us. They will believe again and again that they have come to fight *slaves*.
(HE *smiles*)
They will be fighting *free* men thinking they are fighting slaves, and again and again—that will be their undoing. . . .

16.

MUSIC *and* MOTION PICTURE *credits up full introducing the television program* "THE PLAYWRIGHT AT WORK." *Presently camera picks up the host and* L. H.

HOST
In "The Playwright at Work" we are exploring the creative methods, the philosophies and the aspirations of a new group of writers for the theater. Our guest today is Lorraine Hansberry whose first Broadway play *A Raisin in the Sun* won the New York Drama Critics Award. Lorraine—a pleasure to have you here today. I'd like to ask you why you write plays—why you've chosen to write for the theater?

L. H.
Well, I think it's because I'm particularly attracted to a medium where not only do you get to do what we do in life every day—you know, talk to people—but to be very selective about the nature of the conversation. It's an opportunity to treat character in the most absolute relief, one against the other, so that everything, sympathy and conflict, is played so sharply, you know—even a little more than a novel. And

I suppose it's my own private sense of drama that makes *that* appeal to me.

HOST

A desire to talk to people?

L. H.

A desire to talk to people—and to, I suppose, also have them do what you want them to do ultimately.

HOST

Your characters.

L. H.

Yes.

HOST

Are there any particular themes which concern you as a dramatist? Or is it more general?

L. H.

The human race concerns me and everything that that implies . . . which is the most ambitious thing you can say, and at the same time the most modest too, because I can't think of anything that people do where conflict is born that isn't dramatically interesting. And, of course, it's the role of the dramatist to select which part is the most interesting (and when you don't, you get a very bum play!).

HOST

You said in an interview, I think, that you wrote from a specific intellectual point of view. Is that true? And if it is—what is that point of view?

L. H.

Yes, I happen to believe that the most ordinary human being —to almost repeat what I just said—has within him elements of profundity, of profound anguish. You don't have to go to the kings and queens of the earth—I think the Greeks and the Elizabethans did this because it was a logical concept— but every human being is in enormous conflict about something, even if it's how to get to work in the morning and all of that. . . .

17.

MUSIC UP—*a folk blues out of the Southland: old, haunting, American, and infinitely beautiful. . . . LIGHTS SLOWLY UP. SIDNEY BRUSTEIN sits at his drawing table marking a newspaper layout; he is casually dressed, in his late thirties. IRIS, his wife, enters, slips out of her raincoat to reveal one of those hideous yellow-and-white uniforms invariably inflicted on counter waitresses in luncheonettes—and immediately shuts off the phonograph.*

IRIS
(*Too casually*)
Ben Asch was in for lunch.

SIDNEY
So?

IRIS
He said they're doing a tent production of *South Pacific* out on the island this summer. Casting now. And guess who's doing it? Harry Maxton! Sidney, *Harry Maxton!* Remember, he *loved* me when I read for him that time?
(*She is up and whipping through a few of the hand gestures which signified "Happy Talk" in the original production. Her husband looks up at this for a few seconds, sobers, and looks away*)

"Happy talk, keep talkin' happy talk
Talk about things you like to do
If you don't have a dream . . ."

(*Wheeling and facing him exuberantly*)
Remember—he really flipped for my Liat!

SIDNEY
And he hired somebody else. And you know perfectly well you won't show up for the audition.
(*He is immediately sorry*)

140

IRIS
(*Frozen in the Liat pose*)
You rotten, cruel, sadistic, self-satisfying son of a bitch!

SIDNEY
I'm sorry. I don't know why I do that.

IRIS
Then why don't you find out and give us both a break?

SIDNEY
(*He fans that away dispiritedly*)
Does Steiner really tell you to go around drumming up business for him like that?

IRIS
I have not *mentioned* Dr. Steiner. And I am not going to! I am not *ever* going to mention Dr. Steiner in this house again! *Or* my analysis. You don't understand it. You can't—

SIDNEY and IRIS
(*Together, he wearily with her*)
"Unless you've been through it yourself!"

IRIS
That happens to be true!

SIDNEY
Iris, honey, you've been in analysis for two years and the only difference is that before you used to cry all the time and now you *scream* before you cry.

IRIS
You don't get better overnight, Sidney, but it IS helping me! Do you think that I would have been able to say the things I just said if I weren't going through a *tremendous* change?

SIDNEY
(*Genuinely*)
What things?

141

IRIS

I just called you a sadistic, self-satisfying, cruel son of a bitch
to your face instead of just thinking it. Don't you remember
when I couldn't say things like that? Just think them and
feel them—but not *say* them?

SIDNEY

Which amounts to you paying that quack twenty dollars a
session to teach you how to swear! Lots of luck!
(*He toasts and drinks*)

IRIS

That's not the point!

SIDNEY

I'm sorry. Swear *out loud*.

IRIS
(*Through her teeth*)

For someone who thinks that they are the great intellect of all
times, the top-heaviest son of a bitch that ever lived—

SIDNEY
(*Drily*)

Another step toward mental health—

IRIS

For someone who thinks that they've got the most *open* mind
that was ever opened—you are the most narrow-minded,
provincial—

SIDNEY

—"insular and parochial"—

IRIS

—insular and parochial bastard alive! And I'll tell you this:
I may be whacked up, sweetie, but I really would hate to
see the inside of *your* stomach. Oh-ho, I really would!
St. John of the Twelve Agonies, I'll tell you.

SIDNEY
(*Quietly*)

I am not agonized.

IRIS
Everyone is agonized!

SIDNEY
How do you know this, Iris?

IRIS
(*With great superiority*)
Everyone knows it. *Der—der—*
                (*She hesitates and mispronounces it*)
—*Angust* is everywhere.

SIDNEY
(*Sweetly*)
Angst.

IRIS
(*Furious*)
And I'll tell you this—if I had all your hostilities—

SIDNEY
Iris, where did you get the idea you know enough about these
things to pass judgment on them?

IRIS
From the same place you got the idea that you were an editor.

SIDNEY
Which happens at least to be more reasonable than the idea
that you are anybody's actress.

IRIS
(*Rising, slowly, hurtfully*)
Why don't you just hit me with your fists sometimes, Sid!
                (*She exits into the bathroom. Sobs are
                heard.*)

SIDNEY
I didn't mean that, baby. Come on. Do *South Pacific*. I'll hold
the book for you.

IRIS
No.

(*More sobs*)

SIDNEY

Iris, honey, come on . . .

(*He opens the door—she pulls it shut. After a moment he tries again and she, clutching the inner knob, is tugged into the room.*)

IRIS

(*Flaring irrationally*)

Why should I go through all of that to read for something that I know I won't get in the first place! They don't want actresses, they just want easy lays, that's all.

(*Snarling*)

That Harry Maxton, please! He's the biggest lech of them all. You want to know something, you really want to hear something I hope will burn your little ears off? That's why I didn't get the part before. I said "NO"!

(SIDNEY *has halted and is standing, half turned from her, letting it pour out of her as he has many, many times before.*)

SIDNEY

(*Quietly, almost gently*)

Iris, everybody knows that Harry Maxton is one of the most famous fags in America.

IRIS

All right, then. So *everything* goes with him! He just puts on the fag bit to cover up what he really is—

SIDNEY

(*With proper incredulity*)

You mean a lech?

IRIS

(*With a wild, cornered look*)

Sure, that's how twisted up they are in show business, you just don't know—

SIDNEY

(*Helplessly*)

Even in show business—*that* twisted they're not.

IRIS

Leave me alone, Sidney. I don't want the part.

(*She has curled into a tight sulking ball*)

SIDNEY
(*Continuing on, getting the book and then crossing back to her and kneeling in front of her*)
Oh, Iris, Iris, Iris . . .
(*He puts his head wearily on her knee*)
I want to help . . . so much . . . I'm on your side.

IRIS
I just don't have it. They say if you really have it—you stick with it no matter what—and that—that you'll do anything—

SIDNEY
That is one of the great romantic and cruel ideas of our civilization. A lot of people "have it" and they just get trampled to death by the mob trying to get up the same mountain.

IRIS
Oh—please, Sidney, don't start blaming everything on society. Sooner or later a person learns to hold *himself* accountable —that's what maturity is. If I haven't learned anything else in analysis I've sure learned that!

SIDNEY
Thank you, Dr. Steiner! Look, Iris, the world's finest swimmer cannot swim the Atlantic Ocean—even if analysis *does* prove it was his mother's fault!

IRIS
(*Suddenly very quiet*)
Oh, Sidney, this is all a waste of time. You know and I know that I will never show up for that audition. . . . Jesus, do I ever feel *twenty-nine!*

18.

I am thirty-two now. I should like—I should like a company of friends. Brilliant ones! Laughers and dancers! We might do the twist and then African and then Russian and laugh . . . Ah, how I should like it, a company of friends. For money and fame I would make the exchange. But that has always been so; only now I *could* pay the devil his wage!

145

III ✧

What Use Are Flowers?

1.

Am looking for summer place. Must have leaves and things or perish this year. Sorta hard to find woods-dunes-mountains-seashore altogether. 'Specially if one is very, very cullud. . . .

2.

August 23, 1962

Mme. Chen Jui-Lan
Department of Western Language and Literature
Peking University
Peking, China

Dear Mme. Chen Jui-lan:

I am sure that you despair of the manners of Americans, to say the least—your letter being dated April and my reply late August! But may I rush to assure you that the bad manners do not reflect a lack of interest in your warm and exciting letter. It was my very first letter in my life from China and I am thrilled to be addressed on such an occasion in connection with my work. Indeed, as I read your letter I was filled with a flood of things I should like to ask about you and your work, Chinese literature, China—oh, everything! Thus did I keep putting off the reply.

It is my intention, the first thing in the morning, to drive into the village (my husband and I have recently taken a country home, the thought being that work will be a little less easily intruded upon here among the trees and birds. We have bought a rather nice contemporary house in the woods in a part of our country which aside from being beautiful, close as it is to the bluffs of the quietly magnificent Hudson River, is also fairly historical. "Historical" to a Chinese person, I know, must conjure up centuries upon centuries—but I am referring of course only to a couple. Certain of our great revolutionary battles were fought around here and but a few miles away is the home and work place of one of our earliest writers and fabulists, Washington Irving, who wrote, among other things, the much beloved "Legend of Sleepy Hollow." So it is a great happiness for me to be here and—as I was saying before I got lost in Americana)—I shall go first thing in the

149

morning and put a couple of copies of my play in the mail to you.

You speak of your regrets that the work of American Negro dramatists is not known very well in your country; may I echo that in behalf of the U. S. We are, in the professional theater here, obsessed with the least murmur in the European theater, but the art of Asia (excepting Japanese architecture, flower arrangement and kimonos and an occasional touring Balinese dance troupe) remains out of the ken of even those who consider themselves sophisticated in terms of world culture. The present political chasm between our two nations has not diminished that deplorable state of affairs. But, by all means, let you and I extend correspondence to penetrate all that ignorance.

About your query as to my other works—I'm sorry to say that there are no such. Well, that is not quite true. I did do a television drama. It was for the Centennial of our Civil War, and it didn't get on. The why-nots of this are complicated. . . .

3.

FADE IN:

HIGH ANGLED PANNING SHOT—AMERICAN EAST COAST—DUSK

PAN down a great length of coast until definitive mood is established. Presently the lone figure of a man emerges from distance. He is tall and narrow hipped, suggesting a certain idealized American generality. He is not Lincoln, but perhaps Lincolnesque. He wears the side whiskers of the 19th Century and his hair is long at the neck. He is dressed in dark military trousers and boots, his shirt is open at the collar, and he carries his dark tunic across his shoulders. He is not battle-scarred or dirty or in any other way suggestive of the disorder of war; but his gait is that of troubled and reflective meditation. We come down close in his face as he turns to the sea and speaks.

NARRATOR
This is the Atlantic Ocean.
(*He gestures easily when he needs to*)
Over there, down that way, I guess—is Africa.
(*Turning and facing inland*)

And all of this, for thousands and thousands of miles in all
  directions, is the New World.
> (*He bends down and empties a pile of dirt
> from his handkerchief onto the sand*)

And this—this is soil. Southern soil.
> (*Opening his fist*)

And this is cotton seed. Europe, Africa, the New World and
  Cotton . . . They have all gotten mixed up together to
  make the trouble.
> (*He begins to walk inland, a wandering gait
> full of pauses and gestures*)

You see, this seed and this earth—
> (*Gesturing now to the land around him*)

—only have meaning . . . potency . . . if you add a third
  force. That third force is—labor. . . .

CUT TO:

*HIGH ANGLED PANNING SHOT—MOONLIT WOODS—
NIGHT*

*SARAH, a young girl of about nineteen, emerges [as before] into
a tiny clearing.*

SARAH
(*Whispering*)

Hannibal . . . Hannibal . . .
> (*She halts with a sigh of exasperation when
> her eyes see what they are looking for.* HAN-
> NIBAL *is lying on a little hillock in deep
> grass, with both arms folded under his head,
> staring up at the stars.*)

HANNIBAL
(*Playing the poet-fool*)

And when she come to me, it were the moonrise.
> (*He holds out his hand playfully*)

And when she touch my hand, it were the true stars
  fallin'. . . .
> (*He takes her hand; she pulls away with
> urgency. Smiling he pulls a book out of his
> shirt*)

SARAH

Hannibal . . . Marster find you stole that Bible you be in
  trouble bad!

151

HANNIBAL
What you think I would do with a Bible, Sarah?
(*She clearly indicates she hasn't the vaguest
notion. He waits—then*)
Sarah, I kin read it.
(SARAH *lifts her head slowly and just looks
at him*)
I kin. I kin read, Sarah. . . .

4.

PROJECTION of the playwright in the midst
of a symposium with James Baldwin, Langston Hughes, Alfred Kazin, and others.

L. H.
. . . Apparently it was "controversial." When they asked
for *The Drinking Gourd* it was to have been the first of a
special series for the Centennial by serious dramatists—but I'm
afraid, Mr. Kazin, that they hadn't resolved yet who *won* the
Civil War.
You said, I thought rather beautifully, a number of times
how this question—the Negro question—does tend to go to the
heart of various and assorted American agonies, beginning
with slavery itself. And I am so profoundly interested to realize that in these 100 years since the Civil War very few of our
countrymen have really *believed* that their Federal Union and
the defeat of the slavocracy and the negation of slavery as an
institution is an admirable fact of American life.
You see, all of my life, Mr. Kazin, it has been perfectly
popular, admirable, the thing to do, to write anything you
wanted about the slave system with beautiful ladies in big,
fat dresses screaming as their houses burned down from the
terrible, nasty, awful Yankees—but the system itself—it didn't
exist. So that it is now possible to get enormous books on the
Civil War and to go through the back of them and not find
the word "slavery," let alone "Negro." We've been trying
very hard—this is what Jimmy and I mean when we speak of
"guilt"—we've been trying very hard in America to pretend
that this greatest conflict didn't even have at its base the only
thing it had at its base, that *slavery* was not the issue. You

know, they tell you that it was "the economy," as if that economy was not based on slavery. It's become a great semantic game to try and get this particular blot out of our minds, and people spend volumes discussing the *battles* of the Civil War, and which army was crossing which river at five minutes to two, and how their swords were hanging . . . But the first time that I—that someone came to me and asked me to write ninety minutes of television drama on slavery—which, if you will accept my own estimate, was not a propaganda piece in either direction but, I hope, a serious treatment of family relationships by a slave-owning family and their slaves—*this* was controversial. This had never been done . . . They asked me for it. They paid me for it—and if I may say so, in contradiction of everything that we have said, Langston, rather *well*—

HUGHES
Well, you're of the new generation. . . .

L. H.
—and then I read in the newspaper that some studio official—a vice-president, it's irrelevant which network—

KAZIN
Oh, you should say it's NBC—they deserve the credit. . . .

L. H.
—had attached a notation to it saying, moreover, that they thought it was "superb" . . . *and then they put it away in a drawer.* . . .

5.

FADE IN:

HANNIBAL'S CLEARING IN THE WOODS—DAY

A close-up shot of Hannibal's head and the neck of a banjo. Simultaneously we hear stark, spirited banjo themes. Now the camera moves back to show books and papers lying about where HANNIBAL and TOMMY, his master's ten-year old son, sit. Sunlight and leaf shadow play on their faces while the slave strums and the boy keeps vigorous time by clapping. HANNIBAL concludes with a flourish and hands the instrument to TOMMY who plucks a few uncertain chords as his teacher frowns.

153

HANNIBAL

Aw, come on now, Marse Tom, get yourself a little air under
this finger here. You see, if the fat of your finger touch the
string then the sound come out all flat like this—
> (*He makes an unpleasant sound on the in-
> strument and the boy laughs.*)

Okay, now try again.
> (TOMMY *tries again and the slave nods at the
> non-existent improvement.*)

That's better. That's all now—time for *my* lesson.

TOMMY

Play me another tune first, please, Hannibal?

HANNIBAL
> (*Boy to boy*)

Aw now that ain't fair, Marse Tom. Our 'rangement allus been
strictly one lesson for one lesson. Ain't that right?

TOMMY
> (*Nods grudgingly and holds out his hand*)

Did you do the composition like I told you?

HANNIBAL
> (*Reaching into his shirt with great anima-
> tion—and bringing up a grimy piece of
> paper*)

Here. I wrote me a story like you said, suh!

TOMMY
> (*Unfolding it and reading with enormous
> difficulty the very crude printing*)

"The—Drinking—Gourd."
> (*He looks at his pupil indifferently*)

HANNIBAL
> (*A very proud man*)

Yessuh. Go on—read out loud, please.

TOMMY

Why? Don't you know what it says?

HANNIBAL

Yessuh. But I think it make me feel good inside to hear somebody else read it—something I wrote and that I made up out
my own head.

TOMMY
(*Sighing*)

All right—"The Drinking Gourd. When I was a boy I first
come to notice" (all you have to say is *came*, Hannibal)
"the Drinking Gourd. I thought" (there is a *u* and a *g* in
thought) "it was the most beautiful thing in the heavens.
I do not know why, but when a man lie on his back and
see the stars there is something that can happen to a man
inside that be" (*is*, Hannibal) "bigger than whatever a
man is."

(TOMMY *frowns for the sense of the last*)

"Something that makes every man feel like King Jesus on his
milk-white horse racing through the world telling them to
stand up in the glory which is called—freedom."

(HANNIBAL *sits enraptured, listening to his
words.*)

"That is what happens to me when I lie on my back and look
up at the Drinking Gourd." Well—*that's* not a story, Hannibal . . .

HANNIBAL
(*Genuinely, but less raptured because of the
remark*)

Nosuh?

TOMMY

No, something has to *happen* in a story. There has to be a
beginning and an end—

*He stops in mid-sentence seeing the booted legs of two male figures
suddenly standing behind HANNIBAL, who slowly turns in terror. The camera moves swiftly in and his eyes fill the frame.*

*Stop-action . . . and resume. When the camera pulls back HAN-
NIBAL is on his knees, wrists and ankles lashed together. Behind
him, legs athwart, stands ZEB DUDLEY, the overseer, and, in the*

155

foreground, EVERETT SWEET, holding the composition in one hand and slapping his leg with a riding crop in the other.

EVERETT

Now let's have that again, boy. Did you write this—?

HANNIBAL

What's that, suh?

EVERETT

(*Hauling off and slapping him with all his strength.* ZEB *smiles a little to himself, watching*)

THIS! Did you write this . . . ?

HANNIBAL

Nosuh, I don't know how to write, suh. Marse Tom wrote it . . .

EVERETT

Tommy could print better than this when he was seven! You've had him teach you to write. You have used your master's own son to commit a crime against—

HANNIBAL

Jes a few letters, suh. I figger I could be of more use to Marster if—

A close-up shot as EVERETT'S hand reaches out and takes HANNIBAL'S cheeks between his fingers and turns his face from side to side to inspect his eyes.

EVERETT

Zeb—there is only one thing I have ever heard of that was proper for an "educated" slave. It is like anything else; when a part is corrupted by disease—

(HANNIBAL *tears free;* EVERETT *merely smiles*)

. . . when a part is corrupted by disease—one cuts out the disease. The ability to read in a slave is a disease—

156

HANNIBAL
(*Screaming at him, at the height of defiance
in the face of hopelessness*)
You can't do nothin' to me to get out of my head what I done
learned . . . I kin read! I kin read! You kin beat me and
beat me . . . but I kin read . . .
(*To* ZEB, *as the latter advances*)
I kin read and *you* can't—
(ZEB *wheels in fury and raises his whip.*
EVERETT *restrains his arm*)

EVERETT
He has told the truth.
(*To* ZEB, *coldly*)
As long as he can see, he can read. . . .
(ZEB *arrests his arm slowly and frowns,
looking at* EVERETT *with disbelief*)
You understand me perfectly.
(ZEB *looks from the master to the slave.*
EVERETT *nods and the man opens his mouth
to protest*)
Proceed.

*EVERETT turns on his heel and strides into—and off—camera, as
we move slowly in upon the troubled overseer contemplating the
butt end of the whip in his hand and the slave at his feet, who
understands. SUPERIMPOSITION: the faces of HANNIBAL
and SARAH.*

HANNIBAL
(*Smiling*)
What you think I would do with a bible, Sarah?
(*She clearly indicates she hasn't the vaguest
notion*)
Sarah, I kin read it.
(SARAH *lifts her head slowly and just looks
at him*) . . .

FADEOUT

6.

. . . The why-not's of this are complicated. But suffice it to say, Mme. Chen, that I am now getting back to the business of the drama. I don't know how it is in your theater but here that which is called "success" is treated rather like the second coming and it takes a bit of character on the part of the so-called successful author not to be inundated by all the press, dinner party, luncheon, etc., attention which is suddenly hurled at one. One either spends a great deal of time hiding and making up excuses and writing letters or going to all of that. Consequently its been a raucous couple of years. But I am now back to work here in the woods.

On what? Well, for one, I am working on a play which presumes to try and examine something of the nature of commitment. It happens to be, in my opinion, one of the leading problems before my generation here: what to identify with, what to become involved in; what to take a stand on; what, if you will, even to believe in at all. . . .

7.

LIGHT UP *on* SIDNEY BRUSTEIN, *marking galleys at his drawing table.* HE *looks up.*

SIDNEY

From now on, I'm out of it. Period. My little artsy-craftsy newspaper stays clear of politics, any kind of politics. Why? Because the truth of the matter is, dear friends, I am afraid that I have experienced the *Death* of the Exclamation Point. It has died in me. I no longer have the energy, the purity or the comprehension to—"save the world."
        (*With an internalized smile working the corners of his mouth*)
As a matter of fact, to get *real* big about it, I no longer even believe that "Spring" must necessarily come at all. Or, that if it does, that it will bring forth anything more poetic or insurgent than—
        (*With a flourish*)
—the Winter's dormant ulcers!

(He goes back to work, then looks up again)
Why?! You wanna see my scrapbooks? . . . Since I was
eighteen I've belonged to every committee To Save, To
Abolish, Prohibit, Preserve, Reserve, and Conserve, that
ever was. And the result—
(With an almost rollicking flippancy)
—is that the mere thought of a "movement" to do *anything*
chills my bones. I simply can no longer bear the spectacle
of the hatchetry of power-driven insurgents trying at all
costs to gain control of—the refreshment committee!
(He smiles and shrugs)
So there it is: the final end of boyhood. The Death of the
Exclamation Point in my life. . . .

8.

. . . A second work, which I call *Les Blancs*, is concerned
with a mythical African country where an American journalist
is somewhat reversed in his expectations. And there is also
a third: a bit of a fantasy thing about war and peace, which
treats of an old hermit who comes out of the forest after we
have all gone and blown up the world, and comes upon a
group of children, the sole survivors, we shall assume, who are
quite wild. The action of the play hangs upon his effort to
impart to them his knowledge of civilization which once he
had renounced. . . .

9.

LIGHT UP *on the old man last seen
in the Prologue, kneeling and ex-
amining a spot of earth.*

HERMIT
By heaven! Those are most attractive radishes, Thomas. Very
good!
(Rising)
Come along now, time for class.
(The CHILDREN, *who are all offstage, be-
yond the footlights, moan. He nods.)*
How quickly you learn . . .

(He clears his throat and begins)

Time now, boys and girls, for the vocational section. And all I can say is that primitive though my knowledge of technical skills may be—you had better be bloody grateful that I have at least some. In my world, certain men prided themselves on *not* knowing the things I am attempting to teach you. . . . So, I shall do the best I can, do you hear me?

(Under his breath)

And when you learn to understand what the deuce I am talking about most of the time, you will also understand that you have just had a profound apology for ignorance, disguised as a boast. I was indeed a true member of the tribe!

Now let me see . . . *Ceramics.* (If only we had a manual. Does one bake the clay before or *after* it's dry? There is a point at which the clay must be put into a—kiln? . . . "Kiln"?!) Yes, well, in any event—remember yesterday we gathered clay at the river bank?

(Holding up a handful of clay)

Repeat it: "CLAY."

CHILDREN

CLAY.

HERMIT

Very good. Clay. And I did this to it—
(Holds up clay pot again)

CHILDREN

CLAY!

(He points again to the pot for a further answer)

POT.

HERMIT

And sat it in the sun. "Sun."
(He points overhead)

CHILDREN

SUN.

160

HERMIT

And now, see, it is hard. And now it is possible for one to
carry not only one object—but several. Now this process is
called—

> (*He makes as if he is fashioning the pot
> again*)

"Work." Say it.

CHILDREN

WORK.

HERMIT

And with "clay" and "work," you can make all you need of
these. So that you can "use" it. "USE" it. "USE". . . .

> (*The "class" is obviously puzzled. He ges-
> tures, putting objects in and out of the pot*)

Well, this, I will admit, is something of an abstract concept . . . but it is a vital one and you will have to master
it quickly. "Use" . . . "Use". . . . It is such a vital
verb. . . .

> (*The* CHILDREN *are silent; it is too abstract.
> And he goes through it again. Then, with
> great excitement*)

You *got* it, Charlie? Good boy! Come and show me what to
"use" something means. Good . . . Good . . . Right! You
pick up the pot and put things in it . . . right . . . and
carry them back and . . . take them out! Very good,
Charlie. Charlie has "used" the pot.

> (*He takes out his pocketknife and whittles
> a twig*)

I am "using" the knife.

> (*He looks at them doubtfully, makes a face
> and resumes*)

Well now, children, you've made such admirable progress
that I think you are unquestionably ready to graduate to
an area of knowledge which (sadly enough, all things considered) used to be known as "the humanities." I have a
surprise for you. A "surprise" is something that you do not
know is coming and, in life, most surprises are quite un-
pleasant—but every now and then, there are those which are
pleasant indeed, and they generally have to do with another

161

abstraction which you do not yet know how to call by name, but which you have already experienced—by your nose, your eyes, and way, deep inside you. It is called "beauty." Say it. . . .

CHILDREN
(*Shouting, out of habit*)

BEAUTY!

HERMIT

My word, you needn't shout it. "Beauty" is just as well acknowledged softly as loudly. Say it like this, so the word itself is beautiful—

(*Sweetly, lifting his head back and gesturing*)

"*Beau—ty.*"

CHILDREN
(*In dead earnest mimicry*)

Beau—ty.

HERMIT

Again.

CHILDREN
(*They repeat it*)

Beau—ty.

HERMIT

Lovely. You see, your very voices have this abstraction in them. Now, to proceed . . . Here is our dear and useful friend the pot again. Which, as we have learned, "works" for us, when we have worked to make it. Now, we have also learned that we can "use" it to carry all sorts of things: the berries we have picked; the water we wish to carry somewhere—but, also—

(*He lifts up a little bouquet of wild flowers*)

we may use it simply to hold that which we "enjoy," like these wild flowers . . . We enjoy them because—

(*He puts the flowers into the pot*)

—they have . . . "beauty," They are almost as beautiful as our little Lily, which is why we have named her after them. . . . Charlie?

162

CHARLIE
(*Loudly*)

USE?

HERMIT

What *use* are flowers? Ah, but the uses of flowers are infinite!
  One may smell them—
        (*He inhales deeply and so do they*)
One may touch their petals and feel heaven—
        (*He touches them*)
Or one may write quite charming verses about them (now
  please do not ask me what verses are!) All right, now—on
  to the surprise. I think that it will be perhaps the most
  satisfying thing that I shall ever be able to teach you.
        (*He begins to sing—horribly*)

Alas, my love, you-oo do-oo me wro-ong
To ca-ast me ou-out discourteously
When I have lovèd you so lo-ong
Deli-i-ighting in your company.
Greensleeves was my del-i-ight
And Greensleeves was all my joy
Greensleeves was my song of so-ongs
And who but my La-ay-dy Greensleeves.

        (*The* CHILDREN *first giggle at the curious
        sound, but presently hush and listen, caught
        in the phenomenon of the human voice
        lifted in song*)
Well that (loosely speaking) is what is called a "melody." It
  belongs to a great body of pleasure (well, properly sung—
  it belongs to a great body of pleasure) which is called
  "music." Say it . . . mu-sic.

CHILDREN

MUSIC.

HERMIT

Now try it. . . .

        (*They start to sing it with him—just the
        melody—tentatively at first, then with grow-
        ing conviction*)

Yes . . . yes . . . keep to the tempo now! Good . . .
good. . . .
> (*He is quite carried away, almost exultant,
> as their voices rise and he conducts*)

> The LIGHTS *and* SOUND DIM
> *slightly, but the scene continues
> under—*

10.

There, Mme. Chen Jui-Lan, you have something of my
objectives. In five years, we will know whether I am merely
a dreamer. That may be so. In any case, as things are completed, I shall be happy to send you copies and hear your
thoughts. My ignorance is vast and hungry and I look forward
to correspondence with a citizen of the New China. In that
spirit—greetings!

> HERMIT *and the singing* CHILDREN
> *up full. He is completely enrap-
> tured. Then—*

HERMIT
(*Suddenly peering forward*)
Yes, Charlie? . . . *use?* What *use* is MUSIC?
(*At a loss, he gropes a moment then throws
up his hands*)
Yes, well—*just* sing!
(*Then, smiling*)
Tomorrow—Beethoven's Ninth!

IV ❧

CROTON-ON-HUDSON:
Will Work or Perish

1.

Croton-on-Hudson—*Chitterling Heights!*

August 23, 1962—

Have been here in the country for two weeks. Alone. Herculean adjustment for me with all my fears. But now feel ready for the struggle. Will work or perish. The air and sky glisten; the wind is crisp. The night is like the beginning of a dream that will reveal the universe, so drenched in lucidity it seems. . . .

What shall I do this year? What shall I become? What shall I learn—truly learn and know that I have learned by the time I look at these pages next year?

These trees! These trees! "Lord, I fear thou didst make the world too beautiful this year"—and all like that!

2.

SIDNEY
(*Taking* IRIS'*s hand*)
Listen, Iris. Listen to the woods. There's not another soul for miles, and if you listen, really listen—you can almost hear yourself think. Let's go for a walk.

IRIS
(*Huddling close*)
It's too cold. And dark. And the woods frighten me.

SIDNEY
All right then, let's just go into the cabin and I'll make us a bang-up fire and some of the hottest coffee ever brewed.
(*She just looks at him*)
You just want to go back to the city, don't you?

IRIS
Yes.

SIDNEY
You really hate it here in the woods?

167

IRIS
Yes. What does it do for you, Sid? To come up here?

SIDNEY
(*Looking around*)
Coming here—makes me believe that the planet is mine again. In the primeval sense. Man and earth and earth and man and all that. You know. That we have just been born, the earth and me, and are just starting out. There is no pollution, no hurt; just me and this ball of minerals and gases suddenly shot together out of the cosmos. . . .

3.

August 30—

Was absolutely ravaged by depression and loneliness yesterday. *Ravaged.*

Today—completely different. Have put my mind to the business of not caring about unimportant things; it is my little mental task. We shall see what happens. . . .

4.

LIGHT UP *on* SIDNEY, *glass in hand and quite drunk standing on the couch in burlesqued imitation of a Roman god.*

SIDNEY
Lookit me—who am I? . . . Come on, who am I? I'll give you a hint: I'm not Apollo. In fact, I am not a god.
(*As Jimmy Durante would say it*)
Ignore my stately bearing for the time being and look in my eyes, and you will see there unmistakable—mortality.
(*He collapses*)
Who am I? Modern man: flat on my back with an oozing intestine, a bit of a tear frozen in the corner of my eye, a glass of booze which will saturate without alleviating . . . and not the dimmest notion of what it is all about.
(*He does a vaudeville turn and strikes another especially ludicrous pose. Sings*)
"*Oh, we're lost—out here in the stars!*" . . .

5.

Don't know how to do this—waste of time.

"early in the
morning at
the break of
day; listen to
the
donkey—this
is what
he say: he-haw,
         he-haw,
         he-haw,
         he-haw,
         he-haw!"

**DON'T WANNA BE A WRITER NO MORE.
LAST PLAY.**

6.

September 16—

. . . I sit at this desk for hours and sharpen pencils and smoke cigarettes and switch from play to play—*Sidney, Toussaint, Les Blancs,* and—nothing happens. I begin to think more and more of doing something else with my life while I am still young. I mean almost anlything—driving an ambulance in Angola or running a ski lodge in upstate N. Y.—instead of this endless struggle. I expect the theater would kill me. . . .

7.

LIGHT UP *on* TSHEMBE MATOSEH, *a handsome young African in city clothes, facing his elder brother* ABIOSEH, *an imposing figure in African robes.*

TSHEMBE

(Looking into his brother's eyes penetratingly and then shrugging mightily)

Who cares? I don't care anymore. Why do you care? Dear brother, I have given up trying to change the world. In fact I have given up thinking about the world very much. It happened quite suddenly one day, in Europe. I was sitting in Hyde Park, watching the pigeons, naturally—and it came to me as it must to all men, sooner or later: I won't come this way again. Enough time will pass and it be over for me on this little planet. And so I'd better do the things I'd been meaning to do. And so I got up from that bench, my dear brother, and went to meet the girl who'd been wanting me to marry her for several months and whom I had wished to marry for several months but had not, you see, because of—

(On his fingers, deliberately laboring the enunciation of each specific)

—the liberation, the Movement, "AH-FREEKA"—and all the rest of it. Well, I was, as Camus would have it—

(Laughing a little, a small introspective laugh)

—"a free man" in that moment because I chose freely. *I chose.* And so, you see, it is all over with me and history. This particular atom has discovered himself again. . . .

8.

September 20—

So—the autumn has come and all the attendant mood with it. An unspeakable exhilaration, a too, too moving and familiar melancholy . . . I have felt moods here I had not felt since childhood. They are fleeting and elusive, yes. But they come, praise creation, they come!

9.

September 28—

Have torn up another twenty pages—opened another ream— sharpened another dozen pencils . . . and now? What? They say that one should set a schedule and keep to it no matter what: "write" no matter what. I can't help it—I think that's awfully silly, this sitting down and "writing" like a duty. People celebrate it so much because it makes them feel that the writer isn't quite so precarious a creature. . . .

10.

LIGHT UP *on* SIDNEY *and* WALLY O'HARA, *an attractive man in the middle forties.*

WALLY
(*Smiling indulgently as he puts his arm around the other's shoulder*)
Stay up in the mountains with your banjo and your books where you belong.

SIDNEY
And leave the world—to you?

WALLY
Sidney, the world will go on thinking and doing as it wants regardless. Who's counting? Who even cares?

171

SIDNEY
(*Drawing back*)

I care, Wally. I admit it: I care about it all. It takes too much energy not to care. Yesterday I counted twenty-six gray hairs on the top of my head—all from trying not to care . . . The *why* of why we are here is an intrigue for adolescents; the *how* is what must command the living. Which is why I have lately become—an insurgent again!

V ❖

...A Matter of Nature
in Imperfection

"BUT, THE CHILD SAID, THE EMPEROR IS NOT WEAR-ING ANY CLOTHES..."

1.

October 1, 1962—

I have rearranged the work space after the advice of Leonardo; large airy house (not too large) with small, compact, rather crowded even, work area: desk, machine, drawing board hem me in. I love it. It is as I wish it.

On the wall before me, my photo of Paul Robeson—and Michelangelo's David. At my shoulder the bust of Einstein. At the top of the stairs—O'Casey. The company I keep! But—just to keep things in perspective—I have made me a rather large reminder which is now tacked in the most prominent place of all. It reads:
"BUT—" THE CHILD SAID—"THE EMPEROR ISN'T WEARING ANY CLOTHES . . ."

2.

THEATERGOER
(*Angry*)
Yah, well. Speaking of the drama—what *is* your play about?

PLAYWRIGHT
You read it. You tell me.

THEATERGOER
No, you tell *me*.

PLAYWRIGHT
It's not for me to say—

THEATERGOER
(*Anticipating the words*)
". . . Each person will get from it what he brings to it?"
Right?

PLAYWRIGHT
To be real simpleminded about it—yes.

175

THEATERGOER

Then tell me this: What makes *you* the artist and the audience the consumer if they have to write your play for you?

PLAYWRIGHT

I know what it's about. I told you, my plays have to speak for themselves.

THEATERGOER

But to *whom? For* whom? For whom are they written, and above all, *why* are they written?

3.

LIGHT UP *on* GLORIA PARODUS—
*last seen in the Prologue. A drink
before her, she sits cross-legged,
Zen-Buddhist style.*

GLORIA
(*Pantomiming elaborately*)

Take a needle thus. Peer through the eye. As much as you can see will be a part of the world. But it will be a *true* part, will it not? Therefore, set down what you have seen and call it the Truth; if anyone argues with you, explain to the fool that it is harder to look *through* a needle than to look around one . . .

4.

In life, adequate respect must be paid to the tenacity of the absurd in both human and natural affairs. That drama which will ignore the effect and occasional domination of the absurd on the designs of the will of men will lack an ultimate stature, I think. But similarly, attention must be paid in equal and careful measure to the frequent triumph of man, if not nature, *over* the absurd.

Perhaps it is here that certain of the modern existentialists have erred. They have seemed to me to be overwhelmed by the mere fact of the absurd and become incapable of imagining *its* frailty. (The balance which is struck between the recognition of both— man's defeat *and* triumph in the face of absurdity—may be the final secret of Shakespeare). . . .

5.

The people of Israel, at this writing, are trying Adolf Eichmann. It is, I think, a great if painful moment in the history of the human race. I know that among the Israeli people themselves there is some dispute; natural questions have arisen: Is it right to stir up the hideous memories afresh? Should the descendants and kinsmen of the victims of the Nazi butcher spend such vast sums of money to "try"one whom the whole world already believes guilty? *Nothing* will bring back the men and women and little children kneeling at the edge of ditches as they were shot in the heads by SS troopers.

These are understandable considerations to have arisen. But I feel deeply that the Israeli government is entirely correct to proceed with this deliberate and carefully planned *reminder* of what was done—and by *whom*. Confusion on the matter should be alien to oppressed peoples anywhere in the world—including American Negroes; something will in fact be achieved if black men and women everywhere begin to lose their universal tendency to think "racially" as regards the oppression of people. As is perfectly clear, the Jews, the Poles, the Czechs, the Russians, are white people. But the hardly comprehensible determination of the Nazis to destroy them as "inferior peoples" is anything but conjectural.

Thus we need not sympathize with Ben-Gurion's ambitious insistence that Israel ipso facto represents Jews "everywhere." It may be more reasonable to observe that Israel represents itself. *That* is enough. Its "right" to try a Nazi war criminal lies in the fact that it does exist . . . that by its existence it assumes itself as guardian of what is done "to a people."

For me, there is a strong and powerful current of justice in the fact: a representative figure of Nazism tried on *Jewish* soil. Under *Jewish* justice. By *Jewish* judges. I am moved by the thought of it.

It is about time.

* * *

Footnote: Some scholars have estimated that in the three centuries that the European slave trade flourished, the African continent lost one hundred *millions* of its people. No one, to my knowledge, has ever paid reparations to the descendants of black men; indeed, they have not yet *really* acknowledged the fact of the crime against humanity which was the conquest of Africa.

But then—history has not been concluded either, has it?

6.

October 7—

Tonight am in extraordinary spirits. Believe the last two
years are truly behind me; feel I can do what I have to here—
if not everything. But it all rather frightens me, because I do
know some terrible thing must now fall.

Well, what I have got to learn, with dedication to it even,
is not to worry about things until they do happen. . . .

7.

I do not think that I will forget days spent, a few summers ago,
at a beautiful lodge built right into the rocky cliffs of a bay on the
Maine coast. We met a woman there who had lived a purposeful
and courageous life and who was then dying of cancer. She had,
characteristically, just written a book and taken up painting. She
had also been of radical viewpoint all her life: one of those people
who energetically believe that the world *can* be changed for the
better and spend their lives trying to do just that.

And that was the way she thought of cancer; she absolutely re-
fused to award it the stature of tragedy, a devastating instance of
the brooding doom and inexplicable absurdity of human destiny,
etc., etc. The kind of characterization given lately, as we all know,
to far less formidable foes in life than cancer . . .

LIGHT UP *on* BENEATHA YOUNGER
and her friend ASAGAI, *an African
student.*

BENEATHA

For God's sake, Asagai. Where does it end?

ASAGAI

End? Who even spoke of an end? To life? To living?

BENEATHA

An end to misery! Don't you see there isn't any real point,
Asagai. There isn't any progress, there is only one long
circle that we march in, around and around, each of us with

178

our own little picture—in front of us—our own little mirage that we think is the future.

ASAGAI

That is the mistake.

BENEATHA

What?

ASAGAI

What you just said—about the circle. It isn't a circle. It is simply a long line—as in geometry, you know . . . one that reaches into infinity. And because we cannot see the end— we also cannot see how it changes. . . .

. . . But for this remarkable woman cancer was a matter of nature in imperfection, implying, as always, work for man to do. It was an *enemy*, but a palpable one with shape and effect and source; and if it existed it could be destroyed. She saluted it accordingly, without despondency, but with a lively, beautiful and delightfully ribald anger. There was one thing, she felt, which would prove equal to its relentless ravages and that was the genius of man. Not his mysticism, but man with tubes and slides and the stubborn human notion that the stars are very much within our reach.

The last time I saw her she was sitting surrounded by her paintings with her manuscript laid out for me to read, because, she said, she wanted to know what a *young person* would think of her thinking: one must always keep up with what young people thought about things because, after all, they were *change*.

Every now and then her jaw set in anger as we spoke of things people should be angry about. And then, for relief, she would look out at the lovely bay at a mellow sunset settling on the water. Her face softened with love of all that beauty and, watching her, I wished with all my power what I knew that she was wishing: that she might live to see at least *one more summer*. Through her eyes I finally gained the sense of what it might mean: more than the coming autumn with its pretentious melancholy; more than an austere and silent winter which must shut dying people in for precious months; more even than the frivolous spring, too full of too many false promises, would be the gift of another summer with its stark and intimate assertion of neither birth nor death but Life at the apex—with the gentlest nights and, above all, the longest days. . . .

8.

LIGHT UP *on the* PLAYWRIGHT—*as before*

PLAYWRIGHT

. . . *That is what I said to my friend: I wish to live because life has within it that which is good, that which is beautiful and that which is love. Therefore, since I have known all of these things, I have found them to be reason enough and— I wish to live. . . .*

PART THREE

A Line Into Infinity

I ⬥

The Bulwark of the Republic

DAVID ATTIE

INTERVIEWER

I know that you have said that science will bring more rewards for our generation than God. Does this mean that you place your faith in a very rational, scientific approach to existence *now*—rather than in the traditional religious beliefs of, say, Mama in your play?

L. H.

Yes, I do. I think that . . . well, you see, I don't think anything new has happened since rationalism burst forth with the Renaissance and the subsequent developments in rational thought. We only revert back to mystical ideas—which includes most contemporary orthodox religious views, in my opinion—because we simply are confronted with some things we don't yet understand. So we start all over again with what people were saying two thousand years ago. We say, "Well, you see, because we don't *know* thus and thus, therefore there is some other Agent that we will never find." I don't see how that follows. I think it's simply a question of things we don't yet *know*.

INTERVIEWER

Yet, in the case of Mama, she gets so much sustenance from this—this kind of faith. . . .

L. H.

Well, this is one of the glories of man, the inventiveness of the human mind and the human spirit: whenever life doesn't seem to give an answer, we create one. And it gives us strength. I don't attack people who are religious at all, as you can tell from the play; I rather admire this human quality to make our own crutches as long as we need them. The only thing I am saying is that once we can *walk*, you know—then drop them.

INTERVIEWER

Well, then, actually, you believe in a kind of increase in moral and philosophical strength by the use of reason, don't you?

Oh, yes. Yes. I don't think a time will ever come when we will dismiss the human spirit. I don't think there's any contradiction: we don't need mysticism to exalt man. Man exalts himself by his achievements . . . and his power to rationalize —or excuse me—his power to *reason!*

(*Laughter*)

Well now, of course, his rationalization has its benefits too. I don't know if he could get along without that either.

3.

October 11, 1962—

The magic has come: about an hour ago! A torrent of what I have been trying to write all along. The people I know in the Village and not a stagey version of them. It will be all right now—a lot of work. But I know *what* I am writing now. It came all at once while I was in the kitchen and I wrote fourteen pages in an hour that will hardly need revision I think. Thank God, thank God! I could not have stood much more. . . .

4.

> MUSIC *and* LIGHTS UP. SIDNEY *and* IRIS *are seated as before with the audition book for* South Pacific. *There is a loud knocking at the door and* IRIS *opens it to* MAVIS BRYSON—*an older, heavier, more fashionable version of herself—and without a moment's pause, demonstratively, shuts and bars it with her body.*

IRIS

I don't need it—

(*Meaning the dress box which her sister is carrying*)

—I don't want it—and I won't take it.

MAVIS

Just try it on. That's all I ask.

(IRIS *reluctantly opens the door to admit her*)

Hello, Sid, darling.

SIDNEY

Hello, Mav.

MAVIS

(*Blithely opening the box*)

Could you conceivably have the hootenanny at another time?

(*She turns off the phonograph*)

IRIS

We don't go to cocktail parties, Mavis. At least the kind where you dress like *that*. I want to tell you from the top, Mavis. This is not a good time. I am in no mood for the big sister-little sister hassle today. That's all I—

(MAVIS *crosses and maternally stops* IRIS' *mouth in mid-speech with one hand*)

MAVIS

Just slip it on; I had it taken up for you. You'll look stunning in it.

(*Confidentially, as she zips and buttons*)

What have you heard from Gloria?

IRIS

Not a word.

MAVIS

Here, let me smooth it down on you. Now, really, I can't tell a thing with those sticking out—

(IRIS *pulls up her jeans as far as possible under the dress*)

It's stunning! Now, all you'll need for Easter is a new pair of sneakers.

SIDNEY

(*Appreciatively*)

You're coming along, Mavis, you're coming along. How about a drink?

187

MAVIS

You know, you're drinking a lot lately, Sidney. Iris, I thought you always said that the Jews didn't drink.

SIDNEY

Mavis, I'm assimilated!

MAVIS

Where was Gloria when you heard from her?

IRIS

Miami Beach.

MAVIS

And you weren't going to tell me.
(*To* SIDNEY)
Why can't she tell me? Miami Beach, my God! Is she—?

IRIS

Of course she is, what do you think!

MAVIS

(*Covering her eyes*)
The poor baby. All I can think of is that I am so glad Papa didn't live to—

IRIS

Look, Mavis, don't start. I just don't want the Gloria problem tonight. No matter what else—she is living *her* life and we are living *ours*.
(*She looks at* SIDNEY)
So to speak.

MAVIS

Is she coming any time soon?

IRIS

She didn't say.

MAVIS

When?

188

IRIS
(*Pouring a drink*)
Mavis, if you weren't the world's greatest living anti-Semite
you really should have married Sidney so that the two of
you could have minded the world's business together. Jees!

MAVIS
That's not funny and I am not, for the four thousandth time,
an anti-Semite. You don't think that about me, do you, Sid?
(*Loud silence*)
Why??

IRIS
Now come on: You nearly had a heart attack when we got
married. In fact, that's when you went into analysis. Now
either you were madly in love with *me* or you hate the Jews
—*pick!*

MAVIS
(*Glaring at her*)
Did she say if she needs anything?

IRIS
Now, what could *she* need? She's the . . . successful one.
(*She winks broadly*)

MAVIS
Iris, you've gotten to be just plain dirty-minded.

IRIS
Look, I happen to have a sister who is a fancy call girl, a big-
time, high-fashion whore. And I say so what? She's racking
up thousands of tax-free dollars a year and it's her life so—
who's to say?
(*Having done with responsibility, she shrugs
with confidence*)

MAVIS
That's just a shabby little way to avoid responsibility . . .

SIDNEY
Mavis, will you please go—
(*Glaring at* IRIS)
It makes me very nervous to be on your side.

MAVIS
(*Plaintively to Iris*)

It's your baby sister—how can you talk like that? Sidney, Gloria is a very sick girl. She's not bad. She's very, very sick.

IRIS

Look, Mav, you're all hung up in the Puritan ethic and all. That's not my problem.

MAVIS
(*Gazing at her*)

Is anything?

IRIS

Frankly, it's an anti-sex society—

SIDNEY
(*Exploding: enough is enough*)

Oh, shut up! I can't stand it when you start prattling every lame-brained libertarian slogan that comes along, without knowing what the hell you're talking about!

IRIS
(*With great indignation*)

I am entitled to my opinion, Sid-nee!

SIDNEY
(*Utter matter-of-fact simplicity*)

You are *not!* Not so long as your opinion is based on stylish ignorance!

IRIS

Dr. Steiner says it's an anti-sex soci—

MAVIS

The *things* you think you have to talk about!

SIDNEY
(*Eyeing* MAVIS; *to* IRIS—*cat and mouse*)

Oh, Iris, why don't you tell her the new development?

190

MAVIS
(*To* SIDNEY)
What?

IRIS
(*To* SIDNEY)
Fat mouth.

MAVIS
(*Wheeling to her sister*)
What—? What what WHAT?!

IRIS
(*To* MAVIS, *after a moment*)
There's somebody we know who wants to marry her.

MAVIS
(*Closing her eyes and leaning back as if
some particular prayer has been answered
at exactly this moment*)
Praise his name!
(SIDNEY *smiles angelically*)
Who?
(*Anxiously*)
One of *your* friends?
(*He nods "yes."*)
What does he do?

SIDNEY
Well, as a matter of fact, he works in a bookstore.

MAVIS
In a *what?*

SIDNEY
He works in a bookstore. Part time.
(*Deadpan*)
And as a matter of fact . . . he used to be a Communist.
(*His sister-in-law just stares at him with an
open mouth and then looks to her sister. She*

191

*then exhales a breath to demonstrate she
feels that anything is possible here.*)
But it's all right, Mav. He's strictly an N-M-S-H-type Red.

SIDNEY
(Mugging)
"No-more-since-Hungary."

MAVIS
Does he know?
(SIDNEY *stares at her blankly*)
Does he know what—ah. . .

SIDNEY
Does he know what Gloria does? For a living? No. She told
him the model bit.

MAVIS
(Hopefully)
Listen, people like that, I mean Communists and things—
they're supposed to be very *radical* . . . about things . . .
well . . .
(Pathetically)
Well, aren't they?

SIDNEY
Who can say? There's "people like that" and "people like
that."

MAVIS
Is he good-looking? What about Gloria? What does she . . . ?

SIDNEY
(Deliberately playing it)
Uh, Mavis—

MAVIS
*(Finally giving full vent to the moment.
Her work is cut out for her: shower, ca-
terer, invitation list . . .)*

192

I knew this nightmare would have to end . . . It was just something that happened. It's the way the world is . . .

SIDNEY

He's also a Negro one, Mavis.

MAVIS

. . . these days. People don't know what to do with—
(*Deep, guttural, as at last it registers*)
A *Negro what—?*

SIDNEY

A Negro Communist. Well, that is to say, he's not a Communist any more. But he's still a Negro.

MAVIS

(*Looking from one to the other open-mouthed*)
Are you—
(*Silence as she turns her head back and forth again*)
Are you—
(*Finally, composing herself*)
—sitting there talking about . . . a *colored* boy?

SIDNEY

(*Rapidly, wagging his finger*)
1964, Mavis, 1964! "Uncommitted Nations," "Free World!"
Don't say it, honey, don't say it! We'll think you're not chic!

MAVIS

I don't think you're funny worth a damn!
(*Looking from one to the other*)
What do you think Gloria *is*—???
(*She turns away trapped: what Gloria "is" is not exactly her trump card.*)
Well—well, if this is your idea of some kind of bohemian joke I just don't think it's cute or clever or *anything*. I would rather see her—

193

SIDNEY
(*Finishing it for her*)
—go on shacking up with any poor sick bastard in the world
with a hundred bucks for a convention weekend!
(*They glare at one another*)

MAVIS
Well now, listen, there are other men in the world! The last
time I looked around me there were still some white men
left in this world. Some fine ordinary upstanding plain
decent very white men who were still looking to marry very
white women. . . .
    (SIDNEY *and* IRIS *both meet her eyes blankly
    and at last, hopelessly, she gathers herself up
    and heads for the door*)

SIDNEY
(*Suddenly, with openhearted malice*)
Well, Iris, there she is: Mavis—the Bulwark of the Republic!
The Mother Middleclass itself standing there revealed in all
its towering courage!
    (*There is a snicker of delight from* IRIS; *he
    has lifted his glass to her for these insults.
    Then—dismissal*)
Mavis, go or stay—but we've got to eat.
    (MAVIS *halts and turns back to face them*)

MAVIS
(*She is silent so long that they look up at
her, still with varying degrees of amuse-
ment; then—*)
I am standing here and I am thinking: how smug it is in bo-
hemia. I was taught to believe that—
(*Near tears*)
—creativity and great intelligence ought to make one ex-
pansive and understanding. That if ordinary people, among
whom I have the sense at least to count myself, could not
expect understanding from artists and—whatever it is that
you are, Sidney—then where indeed might we look for it
at all in this quite dreadful world.
    (*She almost starts out, but thinks of the cap*)
. . . Since you have all so busily got rid of God for us!

DIMOUT

194

II ⌒⧓⌒

There Are
No Simple Men

THE MOVEMENT

THE MOVEMENT

Documentary
of a Struggle
for Equality

text by Lorraine Hansberry

I think that American writers have begun to believe what I suspect has always been one of the secrets of fine art: that there are no simple men. Chinese peasants and Congolese soldiers make drastic revolutions in the world while the obtuse and myth-accepting go on reflecting on the "inscrutability and eternal placidity" of those peoples. I believe that when the blinders are dropped, it will be discovered that while an excessively poignant Porgy was being instilled in generations of Americans, his truer-life counterpart was ravaged by longings that were, and are, in no way alien to those of the rest of mankind, and that bear within them the stuff of truly great art. He is waiting yet for those of us who will but look more carefully into his eyes, and listen more intently to his soliloquies. We must not be intimidated by the residue of the past; the world is paying too large a price for the deception of those centuries; each hour that flies teaches that Porgy is as much inclined to hymns of sedition as to lullabies and love songs; he is profoundly complicated and interesting; everywhere he is making his own sounds in the night. I believe that it is within the cultural descendants of Twain and Whitman and Melville and O'Neill to listen and absorb them, along with the totality of the American landscape, and give back their findings in new art to the great and vigorous institution that is the American theater. . . .

2.

December 20, 1962

Dr. Henry David
President
The New School for Social Research
66 West 12 Street
New York 11, N. Y.

Dear Dr. David:

Thank you for your note and, indeed, thank you and Mrs. David for your hospitality before and after Professor Brown's lecture.

I am taking the liberty of enclosing an article, "The Fire Next Time," by James Baldwin, from the November 17th

New Yorker. You may be acquainted with it already. I think it one of the extraordinary documents of our time; perhaps any time. I say this because when I read it it seemed to me to articulate the inarticulable; as if Billy Budd had finally found the words to match his passion. Perhaps it will help you and Mrs. David to understand some of what was agitating those young Negroes at the lecture and in your office; that is what I think that Baldwin accomplishes.

Again, thank you for your graciousness.

Sincerely,

3.

When one reads Norman Mailer on "The White Negro," not anger but a sense of frustration commands. He did not call his essay "The Hipster" or "The Outsider" or "We Who Might Swing" or any of that; he called it "The White Negro." He manufactured an absurdity and locked himself in it. He fabricated his own mythology concerning certain "universals" of twenty million "outsiders" and rejoiced because his philosophy fitted his premise.

One feels always that Mailer is a good man; an essence for whom we might almost hold our breaths awaiting some measure of triumph, because he seems to encompass the possibilities of the true hero whom we await on this unspeakably barren landscape. Yet he is like Seymour Krim *—symbolic of all who fashion their particular fantasies and "Take the 'A' Train" to Harlem to find them, and there meet some fraction of one percent of the seven hundred thousand people who bulge the community and go back downtown and write essays *not* on the prostitutes *they* met, but on—"Harlem."

It is beginning to seem an inexhaustible tradition. The New Paternalists really think, it seems, that their utterances of the oldest racial clichés are, somehow, a demonstration of their liberation from the hanky-panky of liberalism and God knows what else. Yet what seems to trap them is, after all, but another expression of the gross and perverted romanticism in which we all live. Do not Americans constantly refer to their sexual maladjustments as

* Seymour Krim, *Notes of a Nearsighted Cannoneer,* Excelsior Press, 1961.

a curse from *their* particular "Puritanical past" (as if the maturation of sexual attitudes of some kind were not now going on everywhere in the world at one level or another). From Faulkner up or down, do we not show an astonishing dispensation to speak of things being "in the blood"? The Southerner says, "it's just *something* in me," and a whole nation nods. . . .

America long ago fell in love with an image. It is a sacred image, fashioned over centuries of time: this image of the unharried, unconcerned, glandulatory, simple, rhythmical, amoral, dark creature who was, above all else, a *miracle of sensuality*. It was created, and it persists, to provide a personified pressure valve for fanciful longings in American dreams, literature, and life, and it has an extremely important role to play in the present situation of our national sense of decency. For by and large, historically speaking, the intent has been to exclude the Negro as human being from the consciousness of his countrymen—with a certain, peculiar, necessary exception: he was to be allowed to exist in that consciousness, fostered even, in the form of repository of all the suppressions the dominant society found unseemly in certain of its classes. And thus the image was of vicious and wishful intent at the same time. We all know that Catfish Row was never invented to slander anyone; it was intended only as a mental haven for readers and audiences who could bask in the unleashed passions of those "lucky ones" for whom abandonment was apparently permissible. And this was necessary because, in almost paradoxical fashion, it disturbs the soul of man to *truly* understand what he invariably senses: that *nobody* really finds oppression and/or poverty tolerable.

Guilt would come to bear too swiftly and too painfully if white America were really obliged quite suddenly to think of the Negro quite as he is, that is, simply as a human being. That *would* raise havoc. White America has to believe not only that the oppression of the Negro is unfortunate (because most of white America does believe that), but something *else*, to keep its sense of the unfortunate from turning to a sense of outrage. White America has to believe "The Blacks" are different—and not only so, but that, by the mystique of this difference, they actually profit in certain charming ways which escape the rest of us with all our engrossing complexities. . . .

Yet what is curious, what never ceases to amaze no matter how long one lives in America, is that it always seems to shock those without that the Negro is confounded by this image that they have of him; that we Negroes cannot seem to find ourselves in that image. And this has nothing to do with posing one lie against another. People of my generation do not hesitate to say they *like* to dance, if they do, and are pleased to be complimented if they do it well; it is simply not within our frame of understanding to consider this the God-given mark of twenty million. I suppose all of us, too, have known men whom our community, just as much as the white one, has regarded as shiftless—but the simple difference is that we know *more* men who have worked themselves into early graves.

The expression "a frigid woman" is not likely to be a contradiction in terms to us because we are speaking of a black woman.

The individual who perspires freely without benefit of modern deodorants is likely to be merely unpopular, rather than a "prize buck."

But how can Mailer or Genêt or Algren really be expected to know, really know, that the commonplace reverse assumptions among Negroes about everybody *else* are just as touching, innocent and vicious? I know very few "blood-believing" Negroes who are not firmly convinced that the "roots of life" are in Puerto Ricans, Italians and everyone else of "Latin temperament." ("Honey, *those* people really know how to live—" it runs.) Seymour Krim does not understand that when he left the most lowly of the barflies in Harlem they re-engaged in chitchat concerning the most traditional of *very* exotic notions about the Jewish people which, steeped though these may be in the curious quality of "brother-envy," are as grim and unworthy there as they are anyplace else in America. ("Baby, you've got to give them credit: they *really* stick together!")

Must we celebrate this madness in any direction?

Is it not "known" in the ghetto that white people, as an entity, are "dirty" (especially white women—who never seem to do their own cleaning); inherently "cruel" (the cold fierce roots of Europe: who else could put all those people into ovens *scientifically?*); "smart" (you really have to hand it to the m.f.'s); and anything *but* cold and passionless (because look who has had to live with little else than their passions in the guise of lust and hatred all these centuries)? And so on.

None of which is intended to deny or contradict one fact: *of course* oppression does make people better than their oppressors. Apparently that cannot be otherwise; but that is not a condition fixed in time and space and sealed in the loins by genetic mysteries. The New Paternalists have mistaken the *oppression* of the Negro *for* "the Negro." They have found in his *color*, not in his bondage, the source of his grace and wily speech. They are as certain as Genêt that the brooding hatred, which intelligent whites are now apparently able to see, is somehow wedded to the blackness. It is an empty if seductive piece of poetry. . . .

Yet looking back over these thoughts that I have penned here—I am disappointed and saddened. The patches of anger and frequent flippancies do not, somehow, thrust my deepest and most sincere hopes through the window, crash the lock which gives birth to such misunderstanding in the first place. These gentle, if impassioned artists whom I have mainly sailed into are not the "enemies" of Negroes. We all know that; that accounts for the aforementioned melancholy which colors all effort to try and really "talk to one another." Heaven only knows, men fixed in a posture of consuming outrage because of the spectacle of this world have been, as I said at the beginning, "the best of men" in all ages. Genêt, Mailer and Algren are right to be in contempt of the ghastly hypocrisy of their culture; artists who are not are, indeed, lesser artists and lesser men. In any other context they would deserve mainly salutation.

No, it is not the death of his arrogance which I wish for Norman Mailer; I do not know what *humility* has accomplished in the history of man, when all is said and done. The wish is only that the arrogance become not shapeless; that it does not lose confidence in those on this barren landscape who await, with such hunger and need, the words which carry it, knowing all the while its truly monumental possibilities.

Norman, write not of the greatness of our peoples—yours or mine—in the *past* tense.

Because: *"Vail kumen vet noch undzer oysgebenkte sho!"* *
And—*"My Lord, what a mornin'!"*

---

* "Because the hour that we have hungered for is near!"
—from "The Song of the Warsaw Ghetto," by Hersch Glick, who died there.

III ❖

The Bridge
Across the Chasm

December 14, 1962—

Last night set down a drunken prospectus for a Harlem community theater to be named the "John Brown Memorial Theater of Harlem." (Can just hear those Negroes talking now: "I don't care *what* kind of white man he was—!" Well, perhaps it will suffice to call it the Harlem Community Theater.) The plays of us who merit production, borrowing techniques from the entire world and enriching it with an idiom peculiarly our own. . . .

Naturally, in this theater, there should be a great deal of the choral traditions of our people.

Who will administrate? How much money?

It will require stars of course—to get the community to come. There must be no arty nonsense about that from the start, and, it occurred to me, that it means we shall conceivably be obliged to create a particular form of acting—as most of our stars are variety artists. An interesting problem for such a theater. Brecht would have rejoiced in its automatic implications for the anti-naturalistic theater. But would Shakespeare, O'Casey? Besides that, what are the new principles it will need to embrace? In style? Form? Presentation?

"Negro style" seems broad but is, like the Negro dance, based almost entirely on nuance. It is what Pearl Bailey does *not* say that is so hilarious. . . .

2.

MUSIC UP, *the bland Lawrence Welk variety. Background suggests a cocktail party. From opposite directions enter a black woman elegantly dressed in evening clothes, and a stylish male white intellectual. Their manner is brisk, spirited, in high style. He waves to an imaginary guest, she smiles to another, they meet. In this sequence she is both the*

SHE

We spoke first of the Presidential inauguration. "But," he
said—

HE
(*Picking it up*)

—that was Marion Anderson and she *was* singing "The Star
Spangled Banner!"

SHE

Yes—I replied—and she's much revered by me. And the butler
was wearing the most impeccable tails. But there you are.
They're *still* doing exactly what their counterparts would
have been doing one hundred years ago at the same affair:
The brother was openin' doors and the sister was singin'!

HE

Oh, now, please don't get folksy. If there's one thing I utterly
loathe, it is to hear the way you colored intellectuals are
always affecting the speech and inflections of the Negro
masses!

SHE

Please be good enough to explain to me just how *you*, with
your first generation self, who are always, thank heaven,
spicing up your otherwise rather dull and colorless standard
English with old-worldisms from your Mama and Papa's
language—can have the glittering nerve to say such a thing
to me!

HE

Now, now, well, now . . . that's so different, you see. Those
things have such untranslatable flavor. One feels—one feels
one is adding something. . . .

206

SHE

Now ain't you somethin' else? Let me inform you—*liebchen*—
that we colored intellectuals lovingly use the idiom and
inflection of our people for precisely the same reason. We
happen to adore and find literary strength in its vitality, its
sauciness and, sometimes, sheer poetry in its forms. Now
why should that confuse you?

HE

Well, because—because everyone *knows* how guilt-ridden
middle class Negroes are about not wanting to identify with
the less educated classes of Negroes. Consequently, one must
assume that the utilization of street idiom is a self-conscious
and embarrassed effort to re-identify. But—(*triumphantly*)
out of guilt, you see!

SHE

I really couldn't help it. I simply had to rub my head and roll
my eyes and say: "*Now, justa minit there, Sapphire—*"

HE

Oh, now. Come now. Do stop playing Simple. I know the
routine. The trouble is that you've become a racial megalo-
maniac.

SHE

Say, what?

HE

It happens to most Negro intellectuals and artists.

SHE

But you're the one who brings up race every single, blessed
time we talk—

HE

Yes, but you see, you haven't yet found transcendence to more
universal human agonies. Four out of five Negro intellectuals and artists tend to have ultra indifference, for instance,
to the problem of world communism. It's a most sophisticated approach to life.

SHE

First of all—I said (blinking my eyes powerfully)—you don't *know* four out of five Negro intellectuals.

HE

Well, now . . . Ralph Bunche . . . Roy Wilkins . . .

SHE

You don't know five Negroes, period!

HE

. . . Booker T. Washington. . . .

SHE

Besides, why don't you make up your mind about which thing worries you most about Negroes. Didn't I just read an article by you in a "little magazine" lamenting how American Negroes are going to "lose their souls" in suburbia?

HE

Well you see, that is—

SHE

—How we were going to turn out to be just as dull as the rest of the middle class, for the mere price of landscaped lawns, Jaguars, and tuberculosis*less* babies?

HE

Well, now, you have to admit that is a consideration. Earthiness tends to go unnourished on Madison Avenue, or in suburbia.

SHE

And we are so earthy and abandoned, aren't we?

HE

Well, I know none of you like to hear it, but it's true. Now, Negroes *are* different. There's a quality of uh . . . uh. . . .

SHE

Life?

HE

What?

SHE

I know what you mean. No offense. But, look. Please don't
worry about it. First of all, it's not exactly an immediate
problem. But, oh yes, it is upon us: Attaché cases and mar-
tinis! The Ludicrous Scene. We know. But we also know
some of the wonderful things. Personally, I go for chitter-
lings and champagne—which is all the rage in some of the
quarters—you should try it.

HE

Thank you, no.

SHE

You see the fact is we're too close to the horrors of the ghetto
to ever romance about it . . . The Negro mother really
would rather have a tuberculosis*less* baby—than even the
mighty Blues! That's one of the secrets of our greatness as
a people; legends to the contrary, we do have our feet on
this green earth. Oh yes, darlin'! Our spiritual affirmation
of life rests on a most *materialistic* base. How else could we
come up with a song like "Oh, Lord, I Don't Feel Noways
Tired!"
No—I said—don't you worry about us, child. We know where
we're going and we know how we're going to get there.
And I started to tap my foot a little, thinking of the song
I'd just mentioned and its triumphant spirit. Oh, yes! It's
going to come gently and beautiful, like the sweetness of
our old folkways; going to spill out and over the world from
our art like the mighty waves of a great spiritual—

HE

Oh, my dear girl . . .

SHE

I could see his lips moving and knew he was talking, saying
something. But I couldn't hear him any more. I was patting
my foot and singing my song. I was *happy*. I could see the
bridge across the chasm. It was made up of a band of angels
of art, hurling off the souls of twenty million. I saw Jimmy
Baldwin and Leontyne, and Lena and Harry and Sammy.
And then there was Charlie White and Nina Simone and
Johnnie Killens and—Lord have mercy, Paul was back!
Langston and Julian Mayfield coming on the run. There

was Odetta and Josh and Sidney acting all over the place; and lo, Sister Eartha had gotten herself together and was coming too! And there was Ralph Ellison and Pearly Mae and, would you believe it, Pearly Mae had Frank Yerby by the hand, bringing him too!

Oh, it was a wondrous thing I could see. On and on they came, Sarah and the Duke and Count and Cannonball and Louis himself, wearing the crown that Billie gave him before she died. Oh, yes, there they were, the band of angels, picking up numbers along the way, singing and painting and dancing and writing and acting up a storm! And the golden waves rose from their labors and filtered down upon the earth and brought such heavenly brightness. . . .

HE

My dear, you are disgustingly emotional—

SHE

—I finally heard my friend say, and turned to see the water standing in his eyes too, and he patted his foot in the same tempo as mine. *Yes, darlin',*—I said—*sing along, now, honey. Sing along* . . .

(She holds out her hand and he takes it)

HE and SHE
(Together)
I am seeking for a city
Hallelujah
For a city into the Kingdom
Hallelujah
Oh Lord I don't feel no ways tired
Children, oh glory Hallelujah!
For I hope to shout "Glory"
When this world is on fire!
Oh Glory, Hallelujah . . .

3.

December 14—

. . . Now the problem with this theater will be how to develop a flexible truth from the realities of 125th Street. Ours, I suspect, will be a theater *primarily* of emotion. The converse of Brecht: let us perhaps allow our audiences to become *so* spent in the amphitheater that they shall welcome the intellectuality of the pamphlet and the debate—? . . .

4.

LIGHT UP *on* ALTON SCALES, *a young black man of about twenty-seven.*

ALTON
(With quiet, arresting intensity)
You don't understand. My father, you know, he was a railroad porter, who wiped up spit and semen, carried drinks and white man's secrets for thirty years. When the bell rang in the night he put on that white coat and his smile, and went shuffling through the corridors with his tray and his whisk broom, his paper bags and his smile, to wherever the white men were ringing . . . for thirty years.
And my mother—she was a domestic. She always had, Mama did, bits of this and bits of that from the pantry, closet and refrigerator of "Miss Lady"—you know, some given, some

211

stolen. And she would always bring this booty home and sit it all out on the kitchen table so's we could all look at it. And my father—all the time he would stand there and look at it and walk away. And then one night, he had some kind of fit, and he just reached out and knocked all that stuff, the jelly, and the piece of ham, the broken lamp and the sweater for me and the two little vases—he just knocked it all on the floor and stood there screaming with the tears running down his face: "I AIN'T GOING TO HAVE THE WHITE MAN'S LEAVINGS IN MY HOUSE, NO MO'! I AIN'T GOING TO HAVE HIS THROW-AWAY . . . NO MO'!"

And Mama—she just stood there with her lips pursed together . . . and when he went to bed she just picked it all up, whatever hadn't been ruined or smashed, and washed it off and brushed it off and put it in the closet . . . and we *ate* it and *used* it because we had to *survive*, and she didn't have room for my father's pride . . .

(*Very quietly*)

I don't want white man's leavings, Sidney. Not now. *Not ever.*

5.

April 27, 1962

Dear Kenneth Merryman:

I have received a great many letters from students but, I confess, not too many from "a white farm boy living on a rich, fertile farm on the Mason-Dixon Line" and so I was particularly pleased to hear from you.

You ask for my views of the "Negro Question" in the United States, with particular regard to Martin Luther King and the seemingly diametrically opposite techniques of the various freedom movements . . .

I look upon Dr. King's movement as a reflection of the sense of tactical reality which a desperate people constantly demonstrate. I mean that I doubt very much that there is any vast quantity of "love" being generated in the South by the barbarity of racist tactic and ideology. Rather, I imagine that leaders like Dr. King, with their insights into the mentality and traditions of this Republic, have tried to create instruments of struggle which do not lead head-on to the mass murder of our people.

Please understand that I do not mean that Dr. King or any of his associates are less than sincere in lifting the banner of love and non-violence into the winds of the struggle; I am sure that they are. But I am imposing on that my own thought that, given their assessment of the situation, they feel there is hardly another approach. I support them and applaud them.

At the same time, like most of my generation and, in particular, those behind my generation (I am thirty-two), I have no illusion that it is enough. We believe that the world is political and that political power, in one form or another, will be the ultimate key to the liberation of American Negroes and, indeed, black folk throughout the world. It is the political reality of the world without our own shores which even makes the King movement possible, in my opinion.

I think this is what the nation has to face; and, being black and a dedicated American patriot, I am glad. I think that Dr. King increasingly will have to face a forthcoming generation of Negroes who question even the restraints of his militant and, currently, progressive ideas and concepts. The pressure rears up everywhere: I think the daily press lulls the white community falsely in dismissing the rising temper of the ghetto and what will come of it.

In the twentieth century men everywhere like to *breathe;* and the Negro citizen still cannot, you see, *breathe.* And, thus far, the intensity of our resentment has not yet permeated white society which remains, in spite of the headlines, convinced it is *our* problem.

In fine, the nation *presumes* upon the citizenship of the Negro but is oblivious to the fact that it must *confer* citizenship before it can expect reciprocity. Until twenty million people are completely interwoven into the fabric of our society they are under no obligation to behave as if they were.

What I am saying is that whether we like the word or not, the condition of our people dictates what can only be called revolutionary attitudes. It is no longer acceptable to allow racists to define Negro manhood—and it will have to come to pass that they can no longer define his weaponry.

I think, then, that Negroes must concern themselves with every single means of struggle: legal, illegal, passive, active, violent and non-violent. That they must harass, debate, petition, give money to court struggles, sit-in, lie-down, strike, boycott, sing hymns, pray on steps—and shoot from their windows when the racists come cruising through their communities.

And, in the process, they must have no regard whatsoever for labels and pursed lips in the light of their efforts.

The acceptance of our present condition is the only form of extremism which discredits us before our children.

This has been a conversation not an essay and I hope of some meaning to you. If you should care to reply and argue or comment about any of it I would be delighted to hear from you again.

If not, may I wish you a happy and rewarding college experience for the next four years. I don't know what field you are going into—but whatever it is, bask in the opportunity for education, won't you? Mankind has labored a long time to accumulate all that goes into the books which are awaiting you and there is so much that is beautiful and stirring and inspiring in the achievements of the human race that one ought to go through the years of formal education in a state of perpetual exhilaration. And—neglect not the arts!

Warm wishes,

DANNY LYON

IV ⬦

These Thousand
Nameless Faceless
Vapors

1.

January 1, 1963—

For the New Year I have only two resolutions and I know that they are ones I will keep—because I have to: I shall write and I shall train Chaka, my German shepherd puppy. Beyond these things let life bring what it will—

(But by New Years 1964 I know I shall have arranged for different expectations of that holiday. Why? Because I am human and still very young and feel that life—must captivate.)

A few minutes before, extraordinary sunset.

Now rain. No warning.

Human affairs surely are patterned after this thing called Nature. . . .

2.

America as Seen through the Eye of the TV Tube

1. Most people who work for a living (and they are few) are executives and/or work in some kind of office.
2. Sex is the basis of all psychological, economic, political, historical, social—in fact, *known*—problems of man.
3. Sex is very bad.
4. Sex is very good and the solution to all psychological, economic, political, historical, social—in fact, *known*—problems of man.
5. The present social order is here forever and this is the best of all possible worlds.
6. The present social order is here forever and this is the worst of all possible worlds.
7. The present social order is all in the mind.
8. Women are idiots.
9. Negroes do not exist. . . .

3.

Prospectus for a National Magazine for the Thinking Man

I shall make myself a magazine and build it like a brothel. The bricks will be old-fashioned: lovely bodies made dirty by the way

I present them. But the mortar will be new: made of Great Names.

So I will offer Rosemarie and Maryanne simply doing the splits—
But leavened with Socrates on Punishment and William L. Shirer
   on the Blitz.
Oh, I'll show the boys Lucy Jones upside down . . .
But only when she's back to back with a treatise on the excavation
   of an Etruscan town.
It'll be a hell of a clever switch . . .
But I'll prove I'm right—by growing rich!

4.

April 12, 1963—

Tuesday had some weird attack. Almost conked out. Went
to Dr. on Wednesday. Results: Sick girl. Hospital on the 20th.
Enjoying the attention mightily. . . .

5.

Let's face it. The great Race Question has lost stature. The white
man has been reduced to showing that he may be defined as someone who thinks that the names Lumumba and Kasavubu are funny
—and Fanfani and Pompidou are not!

6.

Ball points belong to their age. They make everyone write
alike. . . .

7.

May 1, 1963

Dear Miss Watson:

I am writing this from a hospital bed; they have discovered
that I have ulcers and anemia and here I am. Nothing serious
but enough to keep me out of action for a bit.

In any case I have read your script but determined to wait until I should be in possession of some sort of writing machine before attempting to give you my thoughts on it as my handwriting leaves much to be desired in the way of readability these days.

Your play presented a number of different experiences to me. One of the first of them was. . . .

Interlude—May 14th

I am really so sorry but I had given the enclosed pages to my husband to finish typing for me at home. I am now out of the hospital and here they are.

A final word in summary, Miss Watson: my most honest reaction is that you do not yet have a play. And yet there was that about it which makes me feel that you possess the resources to perhaps try another twenty-five times or so until it says *exactly* what you mean it to. Cruel work? Yes.

I don't know you but imagine that if your temperament is anything like mine you will find things which make you discouraged and, perhaps, a little angry in the above notes. But as a writer I think you will also discern in them another writer's fraternal sense of the pain of creating *anything* worthwhile. And when all is said and done I imagine that you will also agree with me that life has little else to offer other than the confrontation with a problem to be solved.

Please accept my warmest good wishes on it.

Sincerely,

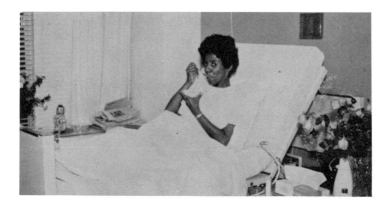

8.

My name is Lorraine Hansberry. I am a writer. I think you know I am your neighbor in Croton and I am very proud of our community. I understand we have an overflow of more than a hundred people *outside* the Temple today.

It is my privilege to be the chairman of this meeting this afternoon which has assembled all of us here in response to an extraordinary mood in our country, to a very great mood in our country, one which now presumes to finish up the unfinished business of American life, the disgraceful unfinished business of American life. . . .

Of the three speakers who are with us today from the South, there is one whose name may by now have some familiarity to you, Mr. Jerome Smith, field organizer for CORE. I think we have all, perhaps to the point of exhaustion, heard of the recent meeting that some people, myself and Mr. Smith among them, had with the Attorney General of the United States. Some of the remarks made on that occasion have been much quoted since, and I am going to repeat one now, since, I am proud to say, it was my own. It was when, during the heat of the discussion—after Mr. Smith had indicated to Mr. Kennedy that the passion and the absence of patience of a sorely oppressed, native American people is beyond anything that we can sit around and be polite about any more—the Attorney General exhibited impatience. And it was at that juncture —and feeling free that I was speaking for every single Negro and indeed white ally in that room—that I suggested that Mr. Kennedy re-examine his impatience, because while there might be in that room some of the celebrated figures of whom we all know—Harry Belafonte, Lena Horne, James Baldwin, etc., etc.—the qualitative change in the struggle for Negro freedom was that we are not, any of us, remotely interested in the all-insulting concept of the "exceptional Negro."

We are not remotely interested in any tea at the White House.

What we *are* interested in is in making perfectly clear that between the Negro intelligentsia, the Negro middle class, and the Negro this-and-that—we are *one* people. And that as far as *we* are concerned, we are represented by the Negroes in the streets of Birmingham! . . .

9.

September 5—

When I get my health back, I really should probably move to Europe. But it's a curious thing: I cannot think seriously of being away from America.

Everyone is always saying I "must" go here and there—Greece, France, England, etc. I feel only that I must go to New England again—and to see the Pacific Northwest and the coastline at Big Sur, and very little else. Man's ruins interest me little in certain ways. I have almost always preferred to read about them than to feel terribly hot and pressured about *seeing* them.

And then too—there is something about doing what everyone else does, the thrill of which eludes me. I mean standing in the Parthenon as tens of thousands of tourists before me have done and thinking "I am here" seems drab and small.

I shall have to find my own ruins, I suppose. . . .

10.

I walk in my American streets and it is such a Sunday afternoon as writers and makers of movies exist on . . . sunshine and the autumn, just hinting that it is almost its time. And the people—some so carefully dressed as to define the day only as Sunday, and others so terribly casual. There is a peace that is supposed to come on such Sundays; it is hard to believe my nation prepares for war.

I think Germany must have known such Sundays. God help us.

11.

LIGHT UP *on* SIDNEY *at his drawing table—with glass and a bottle of pills.*

SIDNEY
They're tranquilizers, my friend—they keep you from getting upset about every little thing. "Every little thing.". . .

221

(Reaching out and taking the pill and the water and setting them carefully in front of him on the table)

Yes, by all means hand me the chloroform of my passions; the sweetening of my conscience; the balm of my glands.

(Lifting the pills like Poor Yorick's skull)

O, blessèd age that has provided that I need never live again in the full temper of my rage!

(Rising, he picks up a yardstick, which, in his hand, becomes the "sword" of the speech)

In the ancient times, the good men among my ancestors, when they heard of evil, strapped a sword to their loins and strode into the desert; and when they found it, *they cut it down—* or were cut down and bloodied the earth with purifying death. But how does one confront these thousand nameless faceless vapors that are the evil of our time? Could a sword pierce it? . . . Look at me, man. Wrath has become a poisoned gastric juice in the intestine! One does not *smite* evil any more: one holds one's gut, thus—and takes a pill.

(He rises suddenly to full Jovian stance)

Oh, but to take up the sword of the Maccabees again!

(He sighs, sets down the "sword," then turns and lamely takes his pill and water)

L'chaim!

V ❦

You're Tough, Mavis Parodus

GIN BRIGGS

January 1, 1964—

Twenty minutes to five. Without: white snow, black trees. The rapidly falling darkness. My soul leaps out of me. . . . The work goes superbly! Yes: Sidney Brustein! His character for the first time—beckons feeling from us! I am pleased. And certain of his speeches now—they transcend themselves and become good language of the theater. I am anxious to get on to *Toussaint* soon—only death or infirmity can stop me now. The writing urge is on. . . .

2.

LIGHT UP *on* SIDNEY *and* WALLY
O'HARA—*as before.*

WALLY
Listen, Sidney, I'm talking to you like a friend. I'm going to tell you something I learned a long time ago.

SIDNEY
(*Swiftly, angrily, as if by rote*)
"If you want to survive you got to swing the way the world swings!"

WALLY
It's true. You either negotiate or get out of the race. Face up, Sid—in order to get anything done, anything at all in this world, baby, you've got to know where the power is. That's the way it's always been and that's the way it always will be.

SIDNEY
How do you know?

WALLY
Baby—I am *of* this world; it's something you know.
(*Smiling indulgently he puts his arm around the other's shoulder*)
Stay up in the mountains with your banjos and your books where you belong.

SIDNEY
And leave the world to you?

WALLY
Sidney, the world will go on thinking and doing as it wants regardless. Who's counting? Who even cares?

SIDNEY
I care, Wally. I admit it: I care about it all. . . .

3.

April 13, 1964—

I know things now. I read of Hemingway in a Paris café writing the story about the Michigan camp and seeing a pretty girl waiting for a date as he drank his Rum St. James and—it is impossible. I am so jing-a-ling with discomfort. It is not true pain, but a nervous unsettling discomfort and I drink on top of the pills hoping to be made sleepy finally . . . so sleepy that it will be greater than the jing-a-ling and let me rest. But so far it doesn't come. Or . . . maybe now it does? Sleepy, yes . . . ?

4.

LIGHT UP *on*—

SIDNEY
. . . A "fool," Wally? Yes, I suppose so. Always have been. A fool who believes that death is waste and love is sweet and that the earth turns and men change every day and that rivers run and that people wanna be better than they are and that flowers smell good and that I hurt terribly today, and that hurt is desperation, and desperation is energy—and energy can *move* things. . . .

5.

In the next ten years I hope that serious American art will rediscover the world around it, that our finest painters and writers

226

will dismiss the vogue of unmodified despair in order to pick up the heritage of a nobler art. In spite of some awe-inspiring talents involved in recent writing, the appointment of sinister universality to Ego in settings of timeless fortune has been a virtual abdication of the meaning of history, which has been resplendent with what may most certainly be called progress. I hope American creative artists will look again and see that Ego, like everything else, exists in time and context, and that the results of the lives of Abraham Lincoln and Adolf Hitler are hardly comparable, regardless of the common properties of that abstraction, the Ego. Nor is this a call, Heaven forbid, to happy endings or clichés of affirmation. For the supreme test of technical skill and creative imagination is the depth of art it requires to render the infinite varieties of the human spirit —which invariably hangs *between* despair and joy. . . .

6.

Ulcer. "Sarah Sore Stomach." (Am in the john. All those people who laughed at John Osborne for making Martin Luther's constipation such a major consideration to the great man did not know whereof they spake!)

7.

INTERVIEWER
Are you trying to find tragedy in these people? In the smaller people?

L. H.
Ultimately I would like to, yes—it's the route that I'm trying to go.

INTERVIEWER
That's fascinating. Would you call your plays naturalistic?

L. H.
I would not.

INTERVIEWER
And what would you call them? If you had to put it in words.

L. H.

I hope that my work is genuine realism.

INTERVIEWER

What's the difference?

L. H.

It's enormously different. Well, naturalism tends to take the
world as it is and say: this is what it is, this is how it happens,
it is "true" because we see it every day in life that way—you
know, you simply photograph the garbage can. But in realism
—I think the artist who is creating the realistic work imposes
on it not only what *is* but what is *possible* . . . because that
is part of reality too. So that you get a much larger potential
of what man can do. And it requires a much greater selectivity
—you don't just put everything that *seems*—you put what you
believe *is*. . . .

8.

> LIGHT UP *on* MAVIS, *arms out-*
> *stretched, in the open doorway of*
> *the* BRUSTEIN *apartment.*

MAVIS

Sidney Brustein!

> (*Coming to him fast, sincerely impressed*
> *and overwhelmed*)

Who'd of ever thought it! First thing when Fred saw the
paper this afternoon, he called me from the office and said,
"Mav, that brother-in-law of yours is some kind of political
genius!" He's so excited. Why, he said that everybody is
talking about you and the paper and the election and the
Wally O'Hara upset. He said that it even went out on the
national news.

> (*She has hugged and kissed him through*
> *most of this. He is vague, distracted, less*
> *than ever does he have time for* MAVIS *now*)

Let's have a drink together, Sidney. I don't know how to tell
you how proud I am.

> (*She takes out cigarettes and lighter and*
> *settles back while he pours drinks*)

I'm glad to have a chance to talk with you, Sidney. Alone.

> (*He sighs and slumps back, arms clasped*
> *behind head, not really looking or listening*)

We've never really talked. I know that you don't like me—

> SIDNEY
> (*Because that remark must embarrass any-
> one*)

Mavis—

> MAVIS

No, it's all right. I know it. You know it. When you come
down to it, what is there to like? Isn't it funny how different
sisters can be?

> SIDNEY

Yes, different. All of us. Everything.

> MAVIS

Yeeesss, don't I know it. I was trying to explain that to Fred
the other day.
> (*A little laugh*)
I don't mean I was trying to "explain" it . . . that sounds so
funny: Fred isn't a stupid man, as we all know . . .
> (*He nods vaguely from time to time*)
But sometimes—sometimes, Sidney—
> (*Looking at him, as the liquor warms and
> frees her*)
—I get to thinking that certain kind of way. The way, you
know, that *you* do—
> (*With her hands, a circle, and aptly, the
> universe*)
—of a whole—

> SIDNEY
> (*Helping her at last*)

In abstractions.

> MAVIS
> (*Nodding*)

That's right. You won't believe it—but—I enjoy it when a person can say something so that it embraces a lot, so that it's in
—in—

> SIDNEY
> (*Staring at her*)

Concepts.

MAVIS

Yes. I enjoy it. I've enjoyed the conversations I've heard down
here. And, Sidney, I've understood some of them.
>(*There is a curious, believable and quite
charming defiance in this announcement*)

SIDNEY

Good for you, Mavis. Good for you.

MAVIS
>(*Oddly*)

But we get stuck, you know.

SIDNEY

I know.

MAVIS

Some of us, we get stuck, in—
>(*Stiltedly*)

the "original stimuli." Some of us never have a chance, you
know—
>(*Wistfully*)

Sidney, did Iris ever tell you about Medea?

SIDNEY
>(*Blinking awake*)

Who?

MAVIS

Medea . . . you know, Sidney, the one who—

SIDNEY

I've heard.

MAVIS

Yes. Well, papa read it to us. Papa read us *all* the classics—you
know, Greek tragedy—

SIDNEY
>(*Looking at her a little stunned*)

Mavis—didn't you and Iris have the same father?

MAVIS

Of *course* we had the same father! What do you think I'm
talking about?

SIDNEY
Rashomon—what else?

MAVIS
(*With her own thoughts*)
. . . and he would read the classics to us, sometimes in Greek—

SIDNEY
You are pulling my leg.

MAVIS
(*Surprised*)
Why? Oh, he didn't really know *classical* Greek, Sidney. Just *everyday* Greek from his folks, but that's what made it interesting . . . we used to do little productions in our living room. He would always let me be Medea, because he said I was strong . . .
(*She rises and bellows forth in Greek, with not badly conceived if stagey classical stance and gesture*)
Ὁ πόνος μέ περικυκλώνει ἀπό ὅλες τίς μεριές καί ποιός μπορεῖ νά τό ἀμφισβητήσῃ. Ἀλλά δέν Χάθηκαν ἀκόμα ὅλα. Νομίζω ὄχι.*
(*Then in English*)
"On all sides sorrow pens me in. Who can gainsay this? But all is not yet lost! Think *not* so.
(*Swept up again*)
Still there are troubles in store for the new bride and for her bridegroom—"
(*Catching herself, sits a little embarrassed*)
Well, *he* thought I was good.

SIDNEY
(*With wonder*)
Mavis, I don't know you.

MAVIS
The ham part, I know.
(*A little laugh*)

---

* Phonetic pronunciation: Uh puhnuhss'meh peh-ree-keek-luh'nee ah-puh' hul'ess tees meh-ree-ess'keh pee-uhss buh-ree' nah tuh ahm-fee-vee-tee'see. Allah dehn kah'thee-kahn ah-kuhm'ah huh'lah. Nuh-mee'zuh uh'kee.

231

I know all the parts—and all the strophes. Sure, Papa was something! Such a dreamer, you know—backwoods poet . . .
kind of a cross between Willy Loman and Daniel Boone.
>   (*Drinking her drink*)
I loved him very much.
>   (*She waits*)
And Fred's no Papa.

>   SIDNEY
It's been one big disappointment, your marriage?
>   (*He refills their glasses*)

>   MAVIS
>   (*Breezily*)
Not for a minute. I knew by the time that Fred and I got
married what I was marrying and I was right. Solid as a
rock. Hah!
>   (*Abruptly*)
We haven't touched each other more than twice since little
Harry was born and that's . . . oh, six years now, isn't it?
Harry will be six next month.

>   SIDNEY
Ah—by whose—

>   MAVIS
—design? Who knows? It just happens.
>   (*Waving her hand*)
Oh, he doesn't suffer. He's got a girl.

>   SIDNEY
>   (*Wheeling*)
Fred?
>   MAVIS
Fred.
>   (*Shaking her head*)
You know, Sidney, sometimes I think you kids down here
believe your own notions of what the rest of the human
race is like. There are no squares, Sidney. Believe me when
I tell you, everybody is his own hipster.
>   (*He digests this, turns back to pour her
>   drink, then, on second thought, doubles it
>   and raises it to her in a half toast*)

232

Sure, for years now. Same girl, I'll say that for old Fred. I've met her.

SIDNEY
(He would, genuinely, like to seem blasé but he can't; he is truly astonished)

You have—?

MAVIS

Oh sure. I went there. He has her all set up. Nothing fancy; Fred's strictly a family man, he puts the main money in the main place, our Fred. But decent, you know, respectable building, family people—a nice place for a single girl—
(The ultimate bitterness)
—with a kid.

(He absorbs this but knows to say nothing)
He's just a year younger than Harry. I saw him too.

(Now she is crying; SIDNEY is helpless in the face of this. She fumbles at lighting a cigarette, which SIDNEY finally does for her)

You do find out. And so, one day, I did what a woman has to do: I went to see. Not the spooky thing, I didn't want to come in on them together or any of that junk. I know what a man and a woman do; I just wanted to meet her. So I got in a cab, got out, rang a bell and there she was. Nothing like expected! Not a chorine or some cheap mess as you always think, but no, there's this sandy-haired kid standing in pedal pushers and an apron, pregnant as all get-out. So I said I rang the wrong bell. And I went back, once —to see the baby. In the park, I had to see the baby. And then, after that, the usual waltz . . . Divorce talk, all of it, you know.

SIDNEY
And you decided against it.

MAVIS

Of course I decided against it. A divorce? For what? Because a marriage was violated? Ha! We've got three boys and their father is devoted to them; I guess he's devoted to all four of his boys. And what would I do? There was no rush years ago at home to marry Mavis Parodus; there was *just* Fred *then*.

(She sits quietly for a moment and then looks at him)

233

In this world there are two kinds of loneliness and it is given to each of us to pick. I picked. And, let's face it, *I* cannot type.
> (*She sets down her empty glass, rises and gathers her things*)
Well, one thing is sure. I don't need another drop to drink.
> (*Patting his cheek*)
Gee, we're proud of you. I told Fred, "Say what you will, but the Jews have get-up!"

SIDNEY
> (*He digests this. Then—in that kind of mood*)
Say what you will.

MAVIS
Now, there was nothing wrong with *that*, was there?

SIDNEY
> (*Smiling*)
Well, let's say there isn't. Today.
> (*She opens the door*)
Mavis, what do you do . . . I mean . . . ?

MAVIS
To make up for Fred, you mean? I take care of my boys. I shop and I worry about my sisters. It's a life.

SIDNEY
> (*Gently, lifting his fists to the gods above; it is for their ears only*)
"Witness, you ever-burning lights above!"
> (*Then to her*)
You're tough, Mavis Parodus.
> (*He kisses her.* MAVIS *says nothing at all.*)

LIGHT UP *on* LENA YOUNGER

MAMA
When you starts measuring somebody, measure him right, child, measure him right. Make sure you done taken into account what hills and valleys he come through before he got to wherever he is.

VI ⊶⊷

Do I Remain
a Revolutionary?

IF I FAINT;
PLEASE CALL MRS
MILI NEMIROFF
PE-7-5537 — or
ROBERT NEMIROFF
LT-1-4320 — New York City

1.

IF I FAINT:

Please call Mrs.
MILI NEMIROFF
PE 7-5537—or
ROBERT NEMIROFF
LT 1-4320—New York City

2.

June 17, 1964—

Monday night was part of a forum at Town Hall: "The Black Revolution and the White Backlash"—Ossie Davis, Ruby Dee, David Susskind, Paule Marshall, Leroi Jones, Charles Silberman, John Killens, James Wechsler. It turned out to be explosive. Negroes are so angry and white people are so confused and sensitive to criticism—but aren't we all? . . .

3.

RECORDING: L. H. addressing a public meeting. Behind the passion and urgency of the voice, there is the excitement, the hum and hubbub and occasional intrusion of a tense, and obviously very much involved, audience.

L. H.

Was it ever so apparent we need this dialogue?
(*Laughter*)
How does one talk about three hundred years in four minutes?
(*She sighs hopelessly and there is laughter and applause*)
I wrote a letter to *The New York Times* recently which didn't get printed—which is getting to be my rapport with *The New York Times*. They said that it was too personal. What it concerned was—I was in a bit of a stew over the stall-in, because when the stall-in was first announced I said,

Oh, my God, everybody's gone crazy, you know, tying up traffic, what's the matter with them? You know. Who needs it? And then I noticed the reaction, starting in Washington and coming on up to New York among what we are all here calling the white liberal circles, which was something like, you know: you Negroes *act right* or you're going to ruin everything we're trying to do! And that got me to thinking more seriously about the strategy and the tactic that the stall-in intended to accomplish.

And so I sat down and wrote a letter to the *Times* about the fact that I am of a generation of Negroes that comes after a whole lot of *other* generations of Negroes. And I said, you know—can't you understand that *this* is the perspective from which we are now speaking? It isn't as if we got up today and said, "What can we do to irritate America?" It's because, since 1619, Negroes have tried *every* method of communication, of transformation of their situation, from petition to the vote—everything—we've tried it all; there isn't anything that hasn't been exhausted. Isn't it rather remarkable that we can talk about a people who were publishing newspapers while they were still in slavery, in 1827, you see. They have been doing everything—writing editorials, Mr. Wechsler, for a long time—

(*Laughter, applause*)

—and now the charge of impatience is simply unbearable.

I would like to submit that the problem is—that, yes—there *is* a problem about white liberals. I think there's something horrible, for instance, that Norman Podhoretz can sit down and write the kind of trash that he did at this hour. That is to say that a distinguished American thinker can literally say that he is more disturbed at the *sight* of a mixed couple—or that anti-Semitism from Negroes (and anti-Semitism from *anybody* is horrible and disgusting and I don't care where it comes from)—but anti-Semitism from a Negro apparently upsets him more than it would from a German fascist, you see. Well, you have to understand then, when we are confronted with that, that we wonder who we are talking to and how far we are going to go. . . .

One of the speakers has questioned our use tonight of the term "Cold War Liberalism." He says he doesn't know what it means. Well, perhaps I can help him. It's not difficult, you see, for *me* to use the term "Cold War Liberal," because it's entirely different the way that *he* assesses the Vietnam War, for instance—

(There is a hush in the audience)
—and the way that I would—
    (Applause)
—because I can't believe—
    (The applause will not permit her to continue)
—because I can't believe that a government that has at its disposal a Federal Bureau of Investigation which cannot ever find the murderers of Negroes, and by that method shows that it cares very little about American citizens who are black— *really* is off somewhere fighting a war for a bunch of other colored people, several thousand miles away. You really have a different viewpoint.

This is why we want the dialogue, to explain that to you. . . .

The problem is we have to find some way, with these dialogues, to encourage the white liberal to stop being a liberal— and become an American radical.

Radicalism is not alien to this country, neither black nor white. We have a very great tradition of white radicalism in the United States—and I've never heard Negroes boo the name of John Brown. Some of the first people who have died so far in this struggle have been white men. And I, for one, would be prepared, I must say in exception to anything said, to accept the leadership of a person who gives that much devotion as against someone who would exhibit the traitorous characteristics of, say, a Moise Tshombe.

I don't think we can decide ultimately on the basis of color. The passion that we express should be understood, I think, in that context. We want total identification. It's not a question of reading anybody out; it's a merger . . . but it has to be a merger on the basis of true and genuine equality. *And if we think that it isn't going to be painful, we're mistaken. . . .*

4.

LIGHT UP *on* SIDNEY *and* ALTON
SCALES *as before*

ALTON
. . . I don't want white man's leavings, Sidney. Not now. Not *ever*. . . . I couldn't marry Gloria.

239

(He takes out an envelope)
I wrote her a note.

SIDNEY
Aren't you even going to see her?
(ALTON drops his head)
And if she was a black woman?
(The question hangs)
That's racism, Alt.

ALTON
I know it—
(Touching his head)
here!
(He turns away)

SIDNEY
(Sadly, looking at him, with sad and bitter irony)
But—"A star has risen over Africa—"

ALTON
(Meeting his eyes)
Yes.

SIDNEY
Over Harlem . . . over the Southside . . .

ALTON
Yes!

SIDNEY
The new Zionism is raging . . . A flame—no, a holocaust in the soul! And nothing is larger: not love, not sex, not camaraderie, not money, not lust. Nothing.
(With genuine, enormous wonder)
What a wondrous oppression must have fashioned this passion. . . .

5.

CROWD NOISES and the VOICE of L. H. UP again.

240

L. H.

. . . I think then that only when that becomes true—when the white liberal becomes an American radical—will he be prepared to come to grips with some of the really eloquent things that were said before about the basic fabric of our society—*which, after all, is the thing which must be changed to really solve the problem:* the basic organization of American society is the thing that has Negroes in the situation they are in and never let us lose sight of it!

I know that you, for instance, Mr. Susskind, are an admirer of our late president. And he presumed—with all respect to the dead, but he happens to have been our president, so I have to talk about him that way—to have suggested to the world that if our foreign policy were not honored with regard to Cuba that he would blow up the world, you see. And we live in a nation where everything which is talked about is talked about in terms of the fact that we are going to be the mightiest, the toughest, the roughest cats going, you know. But when a Negro says something about, "I'm *tired*, I can't *stand it* no

GIN BRIGGS

more, I want to hit somebody—" *you* say that we're sitting here, panting and ranting for violence.

That's not right.

I think it's very simple—I think it's very simple that the whole idea of debating whether or not Negroes should defend themselves is an insult. If anybody comes and does ill in your home or your community—obviously, you try your best to kill him. . . .

6.

> LIGHT UP *on the screened veranda of a missionhouse in Africa.* CHARLIE MORRIS, *an American journalist, and* TSHEMBE MATOSEH *stand looking out.*

CHARLIE

Well, Mr.—

TSHEMBE
(*Turning, crisply*)

Matoseh.

CHARLIE
(*Hand extended*)

Morris.

(*They shake. It is cursory, abrupt; the pace set by the* AFRICAN'*s disinterest*)
How's about a drink? I know where they keep the liquor and it's pretty decent stuff.

TSHEMBE

I think you heard. There is a curfew here—*for natives.*

CHARLIE

I don't think either one of us cares one hell of a lot about that curfew.
(*Pointing to the veranda roof and grinning*)
Besides you are indoors technically.

242

TSHEMBE

Men die here on account of such technicalities.

CHARLIE

(*Simply, looking at the other*)

I really would like to talk.

(TSHEMBE *says nothing but remains*)

I'll get the bottle.

(*He does so and returns; the other stands staring at him*)

CHARLIE

(*Making the drinks*)

I'll tell you right off, Matoseh, that I know that you are standing there trying to decide, trying to pick a category for me. Which kind am I—one of the obtuse ones who is going to ask you a whole lot of stuff about rituals and lions—

(*He hands* TSHEMBE *the drink*)

Or—one of the top-heavy little magazine types who is going to try and engage a real live African intellectual in a discussion of "negritude" and Senghor's poetry to show that I am—

(*He winks;* TSHEMBE *smiles back the least bit, warming*)

really—

(*Wiggling his thumb*)

"in." I am neither. I am a man who feels like talking. Sit down.

TSHEMBE

(*Seeming to relax and sitting on the steps*)

American straightforwardness is *almost* as disarming as Americans invariably think it is.

(CHARLIE *grins and lifts his glass in friendly salute;* TSHEMBE *reacts in kind and they drink*)

CHARLIE

You married?

TSHEMBE

Yes.

> (*Then, to show that the prior attitude has not in the least been dropped*)

I have, however, only *one* wife.

CHARLIE
> (*Lowering his glass, annoyed to be thrust back into the thick-skinned category so swiftly*)

Look, I thought we had decided to assume that the other was something more than an ass, Matoseh.

TSHEMBE
> (*Not looking at him*)

It may be, Mr. Morris, that I have developed counter-assumptions because I have had too many conversations in your country and in Europe.

CHARLIE
> (*A little angry*)

I see that you are outraged by assumptions but that you are full of them. Let's try to get a simple thing understood: I am not a hundred other people. Are you?

> (*They glare at one another; by his silence and hardly perceptible smile* TSHEMBE *concedes*)

Cigarette?

TSHEMBE
> (*Taking it*)

Thank you.

CHARLIE

What parts of the States were you in?

TSHEMBE

Most of your urban capitols: Boston, New York of course . . . Chicago.

CHARLIE
> (*Turning his cigarette about*)

Did you . . . get down to our tobacco country at all?

244

TSHEMBE

Yes, I was in the South, if that is what you wish to know, and yes—

(*Deliberately making this an impatient recitation*)

I did find the situation of the blacks there absolutely enraging.

CHARLIE

You really can't come off it, can you? Why the hell should it be so hard for us to talk to one another, man? We've had five false starts in five minutes.

TSHEMBE

(*Whirling on him, words flying*)

And just why should we be able to talk to one another so easily? What is this marvelous nonsense with you Americans? For a handshake, a grin, a cigarette and half a glass of whiskey you want three hundred years of oppression to disappear—and in five minutes! Do you really think that the rape of a continent dissolves in cigarette smoke? Or the mutilation of whole peoples on a few ounces of amber!

(*He rises*)

This is Africa, Mr. Morris, and I am *an African*, not one of your simpering American Negroes sitting around discussing admission to tennis clubs!

(*He turns and starts out*)

CHARLIE

(*Rather shouting*)

What—will happen if we cannot . . . talk to one another, Matoseh?

(TSHEMBE *halts and their eyes meet*)

You know, I really cannot shoulder my fathers' sins. I have quite enough of my own to contend with.

(TSHEMBE *comes back and sits. Neither says anything. Then—*)

CHARLIE

Did you know Kumalo?

245

TSHEMBE

Know him? I worked as his second-in-command on the Liberation Committee for a year. Yes, I know him well. I was one of his favorites until they kicked me off the committee.

CHARLIE

Why were you kicked out?

TSHEMBE

(*Leaning back, blowing smoke above him*)

They said that I lacked—passion—for freedom. And other things like that. There were several large reports drafted about me.

(*Turning his eyes on the other*)

I am so sorry to disappoint you, Mr. Morris.

CHARLIE

Why does Kumalo support the terror?

TSHEMBE

He doesn't.

CHARLIE

He hasn't issued a statement against it.

TSHEMBE

(*Incredulous*)

He can't do that.

CHARLIE

Well, why the hell not?

TSHEMBE

Because the moment he did his bargaining power in Europe would evaporate. Surely you must be aware that the Europeans have not suddenly become impressed because the African is *saying* that he wishes independence. The African has been saying *that* to the European for generations. They only listen now because they are forced to. And they listen to Kumalo only because he appears to be an alternative. Take away the violence here and they will no longer listen to a man who genuinely aspires to peace. It is the way of the world, hadn't you noticed?

246

CHARLIE
(*Looking off*)
I am thinking of a time when revolutionaries tended to be
made out of idealism rather than cynicism.

TSHEMBE
Maybe that's what botched up all the revolutions so far, Mr.
Morris.

CHARLIE
(*The American*)
Oh, come on now, to hell with all this "Mister" stuff. You call
me Charlie and I'll call you Tshembe.

TSHEMBE
No.

CHARLIE
(*Taken aback*)
What—?

TSHEMBE
I said "No." I prefer to be addressed formally. And, if we
decide to change it, you won't decide by yourself, we will
have to hold a referendum which includes me.
(*Smiling*)
We will vote.

CHARLIE
Now isn't that silly!

TSHEMBE
(*Knowing it is*)
Of course.

CHARLIE
But it has something to do with a principle?

TSHEMBE
Of sorts.

CHARLIE
(*Sadly*)
You can't get rid of it, can you, Matoseh—the bitterness? You
hate all white men—

247

TSHEMBE

Oh dear God, why do you all *need* it so? This absolute longing for my hatred! I shall be honest with you, Morris. I do
not hate all white men—but I desperately wish that I did. It
would make everything infinitely easier! But I am afraid
that, among other things, I have *seen* the slums of Liverpool
and Dublin and the caves above Naples; I have seen Dachau
and Anne Frank's attic in Amsterdam; I have seen too many
raw-knuckled Frenchmen coming out of the Metro at dawn
and too many pop-eyed Italian children—to believe that
those who raided Africa for three centuries ever loved the
white race either. Race is a device—no more, no less. It ex-
plains nothing at all. I would like to be simple-minded for
you, Mr. Morris—
> (*Turning these eyes that have "seen" up to*
> *the* OTHER)

—but I cannot. I have *seen*.

CHARLIE

But you see, then I agree with you entirely! Race hasn't a
thing to do with it.

TSHEMBE

Ah—but it has!

CHARLIE
(*Nonplussed*)
Well now, which thing do you believe, my friend?

TSHEMBE

I believe in the recognition of devices *as devices*—but I also
believe in the reality of those devices. In one century men
choose to hide their conquests under religion, in another
under race. So you and I may recognize the fraudulence of
the device in both cases, but the fact remains that a man
who has a sword run through him because he will not become a Moslem or a Christian—or who is lynched in Mississippi or Zatembe because he is black—is suffering the utter
reality of that device of conquest. And it is pointless to
pretend that it doesn't *exist*—merely because it is a lie. . . .

7.

June 17, 1964—

Do I remain a revolutionary? Intellectually—without a doubt. But am I prepared to give my body to the struggle or even my *comforts?* This is what I puzzle about.

Am now sitting thinking about many things. All the narrowness and selfishness of this last year of my life seems to crowd in on me. I have just finished reading an article on Harlem in the current "Look" and hardly feel that my existence is justified, let alone the "style" of life I lead. . . .

8.

"The Ad Hoc Committee on Triple Revolution" has just put out a 27-page document on the condition of the American economy and society which is breathtaking. It is breathtaking because it summarizes the reality *now. Eight million* Americans permanently unemployed and not about to be made employable by any of the patchwork politics now being thrown around by the Johnson administration.

They call for the universal right of *income* in America!

It is, to say the least, a revolutionary demand. A correct one, a thrilling one. Technology has not waited for our socio-psychological adjustment for even those like me. *The time of superabundance is here.*

The mind entirely flips over in the face of such pronouncements. They are indisputable. They are the articulation of the former mere expectations of generations of prophets of human destiny. But to have it here—and to have to deal with it—shakes one and all the conventions on which one's life is built. Labor, "sacred Labor" —is *not!*

9.

July 17—

Have the feeling I should throw myself back into the movement. Become a human being again.

But that very impulse is immediately flushed with a thousand vacillations and forbidding images. I see myself lying in a pool of perspiration in a dark tenement room recalling Croton and the trees and longing for death—

Comfort has come to be its own corruption. I think of lying without a painkiller in pain. In all the young years no such image ever occurred to me. I rather *looked forward* to going to jail once. Now I can hardly imagine surviving it at all. Comfort. Apparently I have sold my soul for it.

I think when I get my health back I shall go into the South to find out what kind of revolutionary I am. . . .

VII ❧

To Be Young,
Gifted and Black

GIN BRIGGS

1.

1964 will be work. *Glorious work!* I will finish *Sidney* than *Les Blancs* then on to *Toussaint* and LaFarge's *Laughing Boy*—my first musical! *All* this winter.

And this Spring I shall—what? Maybe go see the California Coast—maybe go to Scotland?

And 1965? I will be 35 then—grayer—but alive? I have set no goals in my life and accomplished none. . . .

2.

PROJECTION of L. H. in the midst of an interview

L. H.

. . . My dream? It's largely outside of myself. Which is a happy thing to be able to say. I don't feel especially compulsive about keeping up with anything or anybody in terms of career or anything like that. I really think I am in the process of living my dream. I'm able to work freely and with not a great deal of insecurity and to do the things I want to do. So that there isn't anything aspirational in that sense. . . .

3.

July 28, 1964—

Dr. Warren called last night. I am to go to Boston on Friday. To Lahey Clinic. *There is something wrong with my intestinal system.* . . .

4.

The interview continues

L. H.

. . . I would like very much to live in a world where some of the more monumental problems could at least be solved; I'm thinking, of course, of peace. That is, we don't fight. Nobody fights. We get rid of all the little bombs—and the big bombs. . . .

5.

LIGHT UP *on* THE HERMIT. *He is lying down, weakened by illness but clearly still very much himself, as suddenly he raises himself with anger*

HERMIT

Flowers! Do not bring me flowers, Charlie—if you got hungry enough you'd kill me and eat me! Go away. I've had enough. Of men of whatever shape or age. I do not want flowers, music, or poetry. You want to know why? Well, because you are *human*. You've barely learned to make a pot and already you are fighting over what to put in it!

No, no, don't say you're sorry. Don't apologize and don't say you'll do better next time—because you won't. It's finished . . . our little adventure among the stars. I have been indulging myself, no more. Engaging in a timeless vanity of man. Pretending with you that it would be possible. Pretending that *you* wild little things could conceivably raise Egypt again, claim the perceptions of Copernicus and Newton—ha! of Shakespeare and Einstein! Pretending that I could hand to you the residue, badly learned and hardly retained, of—five thousand years of glory!

(*Turning gruffly away*)

—on which I turned my back with all the petulance of our kind.

(*Turning back and shouting*)

Go away Charlie. It's over! I have decided to die and I prefer to die alone. Ah, you still don't know what *that* is, do you? WELL: YOU JUST STAND THERE AND WATCH!

(*He lies back—and then, relenting*)

Charlie . . . When it does happen—

(*Slowly, seriously*)

and it will be soon now . . . not tonight, but soon enough . . . I will get cold and stiff and still and it will seem strange to you that . . . I ever moved at all. It will seem then, boy, that I was . . . a miracle . . . but it will happen. Because

I am old and sick and worn out—and mortal. But what you have to know is this: when it does happen you will all stand for a long time with your mouths hanging open with wonder. That's all right, boy, it's an awesome thing; it is in the nature of men to take life for granted. Only the *absence* of life will seem to you the miracle, the greatest miracle—and by the time you understand that it should be the other way around, well . . .

(*Smiling the least bit*)

Charlie, you think it's a joke! Well, boy, it really isn't a joke. Some men, in my time, spent whole lifetimes writing books trying to prove that it was, but it 'tisn't . . .

(*Dismissing the mood*)

The thing that you have to know, boy, when it happens, is that after a while I shall begin to exude a horrid odor and what you must all do is to dig the deepest hole that you possibly can and put me in it. It doesn't matter which way and I don't have to be wrapped in anything, I shall be glad enough to merge, atom for atom, with the earth again. Ah, you are wondering how will I *get out?* I won't. I will stay there forever. For always.

(*Shouting irritably*)

Well, you've seen other things *die!* The birds, the fish we eat. They don't come back, do they! The wood we burn, it doesn't come back! Nothing comes back!

(*Looking at* CHARLIE's *obviously puzzled eyes*)

You are thinking that I am not a bird or a fish or a piece of wood. All right, I am not—

(*Smiling slightly and, with a gesture, ending the matter*)

Well, put a stone over my head and come and spend hours there pretending to have dialogues with me and you will feel better. It won't mean a thing to me, but you will feel better. . . .

6.

Health: not good. Continue to lose weight. Down to 107. Poor appetite. Much pain in shoulders again. Stomach cramps, severe, after eating. Frankly, things look rather poor. And the truth is that I am so tired of hurting at this point that I wouldn't mind something rather drastic. I feel as if I am being sucked away. . . .

*Down the aisle and onto the stage
now strides* THE PLAYWRIGHT

PLAYWRIGHT

Ladies and gentlemen, Fellow Writers:

I have had an opportunity to read three of the winning compositions in this United Negro College Fund contest—and it is clear I am addressing fellow writers indeed.

(*Looking about in turn at each of the presumed three in the audience*)

Miss Purvis, Miss Yeldell and Mr. Lewis—I commend you and add my personal congratulations to the awards of the afternoon.

Apart from anything else, I wanted to be able to come here and speak with you on this occasion because you are young, gifted and black. In the month of May in the year 1964, I, for one, can think of no more dynamic combination that a person might be.

The Negro writer stands surrounded by the whirling elements of this world. He stands neither on a fringe nor utterly involved: the prime observer waiting poised for inclusion.

O, the things that we have learned in this unkind house that we have to tell the world about!

Despair? Did someone say despair was a question in the world? Well then, listen to the sons of those who have known little else if you wish to know the resiliency of this thing you would so quickly resign to mythhood, this thing called the human spirit. . . .

Life? Ask those who have tasted of it in pieces rationed out by enemies.

Love? Ah, ask the troubadors who come from those who have loved when all reason pointed to the uselessness and foolhardiness of love. Perhaps we shall be the teachers when it is done. Out of the depths of pain we have thought to be our sole heritage in this world—O, we know about love!

And that is why I say to *you* that, though it be a thrilling and marvelous thing to be merely young and gifted in such times, it is doubly so, doubly dynamic—to be young, gifted *and black*.

Look at the work that awaits you!

Write if you will: but write about the world as it is and as you think it *ought* to be and must be—if there is to be a world.

Write about all the things that men have written about since the beginning of writing and talking—but write *to a point.* Work hard at it, *care* about it.

Write about *our people:* tell their story. You have something glorious to draw on begging for attention. Don't pass it up. *Use* it.

Good luck to you. This Nation needs your gifts.

Perfect them!

8.

Mid-March, 1952 (on board an airplane)—

And so the sun will pass away—die away. Tones of blue—of deep quiet—lovely blue—float down and all the people's voices seem to grow quiet—quiet.

And I remember all the twilights I have ever known—they float across my eyes.

I think of forests and picnics—of being very warm in something cotton. Of smelling the earth—and loving life.

Long live good life! And beauty . . . and love!

BERNARD COLE

VIII ⬦

Before 'Tis Done...

1.

[Undated]—

If anything should happen—before 'tis done—may I trust that all commas and periods will be placed and someone will complete my thoughts—

This last should be the least difficult—since there are so many who think as I do—

Postscript:

Some Background to the Book

and

a Note on the Stage Play

TO BE YOUNG, GIFTED AND BLACK

To Be Young, Gifted and Black was originally conceived not in its present form, but as a work for the stage.

As had been the case with *A Raisin in the Sun*, however (and every other black play that I have ever heard of), established producers evinced skepticism—in this case that sufficient public interest could exist in the life of a deceased playwright whose entire reputation rested on two plays. It remained for a small, decidedly nonprofit FM radio station to provide the play's first impetus; for a giant public institution to become its first sponsor; for a black and white producing team, largely financed by Harry Belafonte, to see it to the stage; and for the combination of an inspired toy distributor and a doctor who doubles as a night club owner, to keep it there.

At a time when, after a year and a half of trying, virtually no interest in the posthumous work of Lorraine Hansberry seemed to exist in the commercial theater or other media, I was approached by Ted Rubin, a volunteer producer for radio station WBAI, who indicated the station's desire to commemorate the second anniversary of the playwright's death with a program of some sort—were there any tapes of Lorraine in existence? or perhaps might a few of her theatrical associates like to read from her works? This presented the first opportunity to place Lorraine Hansberry before the public again in dramatic and meaningful form. Letters were sent out requesting participation, phone calls followed, and the response from the theater community went beyond any bounds that the station, or even I, could have anticipated.

263

The resulting broadcast, *Lorraine Hansberry In Her Own Words*, three months in the taping, writing, and editing, was presented in two parts totalling seven-and-one-half hours, with a distinguished cast of 61, unprecedented in radio history.* The WBAI program afforded me a chance to explore the inherent possibilities of the material with some of the foremost artists in our country, and the wide public response to the broadcasts served as a catalyst to all that has happened since.

Jules Irving, Director of the Repertory Company of Lincoln Center, was the first producer to recognize the potentials of *To Be Young, Gifted and Black* as a play. That was in the fall of 1967. Under his auspices I completed a first draft of the script in consultation with Alvin Epstein, the noted actor, who was to make his directorial debut with the play. Public institutions, however, have their problems too; for a variety of reasons too complicated to go into here—and largely beyond the control of anyone—the play was "postponed" two days before the scheduled start of rehearsals, and presently dropped.

It was at this point that the idea for the present volume began to take shape. Work on the script had produced a form that seemed to lend itself with equal facility to the printed page, while going far beyond the inherent limitations of the stage in the depth and range, degree of nuance and the possibilities for amplification that book form would permit. Thus, work on the book and revisions of the script proceeded concurrently, each drawing upon the experiences and creative discoveries of the other, but ultimately diverging quite drastically in method, structure and, of course, fullness of treatment.

In the spring of 1968 producers Edgar Lansbury and Harry Belafonte joined forces to present the play and, in October, rehearsals began under the direction of Gene Frankel, one of our

---

* The participating artists were: Ben Aliza, Anne Bancroft, Lauren Bacall, Ralph Bellamy, Herschel Bernardi, Theodore Bikel, Claire Bloom, Roscoe Lee Browne, Morris Carnovsky, Godfrey Cambridge, Howland Chamberlin, Lee J. Cobb, Howard DaSilva, Bette Davis, Ruby Dee, Gabriel Dell, Colleen Dewhurst, Melvyn Douglas, Alvin Epstein, Frances Foster, Gloria Foster, Al Freeman, Jr., Will Geer, Jack Gilford, Louis Gossett, Julie Harris, Rosemary Harris, Uta Hagen, June Havoc, John Heffernan, James Earl Jones, Anne Jackson, Angela Lansbury, Rosetta LeNoire, E. G. Marshall, Elaine May, Claudia McNeil, Rita Moreno, Rosemary Murphy, Geraldine Page, Shauneille Perry, Sidney Poitier, Leslie Rivers, Paul Robeson, Diana Sands, Harold Scott, Madeleine Sherwood, Maureen Stapleton, Rod Steiger, Louise Stubbs, Barbara Ann Teer, Cicely Tyson, Rip Torn, Eli Wallach, Douglas Turner Ward, Teresa Wright. The two broadcasts were narrated by Ossie Davis and Harold Scott.

theater's most gifted artists, who made invaluable contributions not only in the staging, but in some instances, to its ultimate form and concept.

TO BE YOUNG, GIFTED AND BLACK *was presented by Harry Belafonte/Chiz Schultz and Edgar Lansbury, in association with Robert Nemiroff, at the Cherry Lane Theatre in New York City January 2, 1969, with the following cast:*

(In alphabetical order)

BARBARA BAXLEY	JOHN BEAL
RITA GARDNER	GERTRUDE JEANETTE
JANET LEAGUE	STEPHEN STRIMPELL
CICELY TYSON	ANDRE WOMBLE

Directed by

GENE FRANKEL

Designed by	*Lighting by*
Merrill Sindler	Barry Arnold
Musical Coordinator	*Photographic Effects*
William Eaton	Stuart Bigger
Sound Design & Production Stage Manager	*Production Consultant*
Gigi Cascio	Charlotte Zaltzberg

Other actors who have since appeared in the play are: Ed Bernard, Alice Borden, Rosemary D'Angelis, Clifton Davis, Micki Grant, Moses Gunn, Bruce Hall, Josephine Lemmo, Bill McLucky, Tina Sattin, Louise Stubbs, William Suplee, Dolores Sutton, and Bernard Ward.

On March 2, 1969, a new producing team—Dr. Burt D'Lugoff, one of "the committed" to whom Lorraine Hansberry dedicated her second play; Ray Larsen, a business man of many parts, who had been deeply affected by the playwright's words; and the undersigned—took over the production.

At this writing *To Be Young, Gifted and Black*, the longest running new play of the 1968-69 off-Broadway season, is entering its seventh consecutive month at the Cherry Lane. On July 1st it will open the Stanford University Drama Festival of off-Broadway Hits.

In 1970-71 a national road tour will be presented. Tour arrangements are being handled by Review Presentations, an arm of the New York Review of Books.

An acting edition, for local and amateur productions, is to be published by Samuel French.

June, 1969   R. N.